Santa's Favorites

Favorite
Holiday Treats
and Christmas Sweets

© Stephanie Stouffer

Published by CQ Products
Waverly, IA 50677

Distributed By:
Giftco Inc.

Santa's Favorite Holiday Treats & Christmas Sweets
ISBN 1-56383-165-1
Item #7040

Table of Contents

Favorite Recipes

Recipe Name	Page

Santa's Favorite

Beverages

Hot Buttered
Drink Mix

Makes 15 servings

1 C. unsalted butter, softened
1-16 oz. pkg. confectioners'
   sugar, sifted

1 lb. light brown sugar,
   packed
1 qt. vanilla ice cream,
   softened

In a large bowl, cream the butter and the sugars together until smooth. Add the softened ice cream and mix until a creamy consistency is obtained. Transfer mix to a freezer container with a tight fitting lid. Store in the freezer for up to 1 month.

To serve, place 2 heaping tablespoons of the frozen mix in a highball glass or coffee mug. Add 1/2 to 1 teaspoon rum extract. Add 6 ounces of boiling water and stir until the mixture is melted. Sprinkle with cinnamon or nutmeg.

Candy Cane Cocoa

Makes 4 (8-ounce) servings

4 C. milk
3-1 oz. squares semisweet
   chocolate, chopped
4 small peppermint candy canes

4 peppermint candy
   canes, crushed
1 C. whipped cream

In a saucepan, heat milk until hot, but not boiling. Whisk in the chopped chocolate and crushed peppermint candies until melted and smooth. Pour hot cocoa into four mugs and garnish with whipped cream. Serve each with a candy cane stirring stick.

Serve hot chocolate with a candy cane instead of a spoon for a minty flavor and fewer dishes.

Perfect Hot Cocoa

Makes 1 (8-ounce) serving

2 T. sugar
2 tsp. cocoa
Dash salt

1 C. milk
1/4 tsp. vanilla extract

Mix sugar, cocoa and salt in a large mug. Heat milk in microwave at high for 1 1/2 minutes or until hot. Gradually add hot milk to cocoa mixture in mug, stirring until well blended. Stir in vanilla.

Hot Butterscotch Cocoa

Makes 1 (8-ounce) serving

**1-1 oz. env. instant hot
   chocolate mix**
1 C. milk

1 tsp. butterscotch extract

Heat milk in microwave on high for 1 1/2 minutes or until
hot. In a mug, dissolve instant hot chocolate mix with hot
milk. Stir in butterscotch extract.

Hot Cranberry Tea

Makes 14 (8-ounce) servings

3 1/2 qts. water
1-12 oz. pkg. cranberries
2 C. sugar
2 oranges, juiced

2 lemons, juiced
12 whole cloves
2 cinnamon sticks

In a large pot, combine water and cranberries. Bring to a boil, reduce heat and simmer for 30 minutes. Add sugar, orange juice, lemon juice, cloves and cinnamon sticks. Cover and let steep for 1 hour. Transfer to slow cooker to keep tea warm while serving.

Eggnog Coffee

Makes 4 (7-ounce) servings

1/4 C. ground coffee   **2 1/2 C. cold water**
1/4 tsp. nutmeg   **1 C. eggnog, warmed**
2 T. sugar   **Whipped topping**

Place coffee in the filter of a coffee maker brew basket;
sprinkle with nutmeg. Place sugar in empty coffee pot. Add
water to coffee maker and brew coffee. When brewing is
complete, stir in eggnog. Serve immediately. Top each serving
with a dollop of whipped topping and, if desired, garnish with
a light sprinkle of additional nutmeg.

Spiced Holiday Coffee

Makes 3 (8-ounce) servings

1/3 C. ground coffee   **1/4 C. orange marmalade**
1/2 tsp. cinnamon   **3 C. cold water**
1/8 tsp. ground cloves

Place coffee, cinnamon and cloves in the filter of a coffee maker. Place marmalade in empty coffee pot. Add water to coffee maker and brew coffee. When brewing is complete, stir until well mixed then serve.

Caramel Coffee

Makes 6 (6-ounce) servings

1/2 C. caramel dessert
   topping
6 T. ground coffee
4 1/2 C. cold water

Whipped topping
Chopped chocolate-
   covered toffee

Place caramel dessert topping in empty coffee pot. Place ground coffee in the filter of a coffee maker and prepare coffee with cold water. When brewing is complete, stir until well mixed. Top each serving with whipped topping and chopped chocolate-covered toffee, if desired.

Cinnamon Spiced Coffee

Makes 6 (8-ounce) servings

2/3 C. ground coffee
1 tsp. cinnamon
6 C. cold water

1/4 C. granulated sugar or
firmly packed brown
sugar

Place coffee and cinnamon in the filter of a coffee maker. Place sugar in empty coffee pot. Prepare coffee with cold water. When brewing is complete, stir until well mixed. Serve immediately.

Harvest Coffee Cider

Makes 4 (8-ounce) servings

1/4 C. ground coffee

1/4 tsp. cinnamon

1/4 C. firmly packed brown sugar

1 C. apple juice

3 C. cold water

Place coffee in the filter of a coffee maker. Sprinkle coffee with cinnamon. Place sugar and apple juice in empty coffee pot. Add water to coffee maker and brew. When brewing is complete, stir until well mixed.

11

Hot Apple Cider

Makes 6 (8-ounce) servings

6 C. apple cider
1/4 C. real maple syrup
2 cinnamon sticks
6 whole cloves

6 whole allspice berries
1 orange peel, cut into
  strips
1 lemon peel, cut into
  strips

Pour the apple cider and maple syrup into a large stainless steel saucepan. Place the cinnamon sticks, cloves, allspice, berries, orange peel and lemon peel in the center of a cheesecloth; fold up the sides of the cheesecloth to enclose the bundle, then tie it up with kitchen string. Drop the spice bundle into the cider mixture. Heat over medium heat for 5 to 10 minutes or until the cider is very hot, but not boiling. Remove cider from the heat. Discard the spice bundle. Ladle cider into mugs, adding a cinnamon stick to each serving, if desired.

Hot Spiced Cranberry Cider

Makes 12 (8-ounce) servings

2 qts. apple cider
6 C. cranberry juice
1/4 C. packed brown sugar

4 cinnamon sticks
1 1/2 tsp. whole cloves
1 lemon, thinly sliced

In a large pot, combine apple cider, cranberry juice, brown sugar, cinnamon sticks, cloves and lemon slices. Bring to a boil, reduce heat and simmer for 15 to 20 minutes. With a slotted spoon, remove cinnamon sticks, cloves and lemon slices. Transfer to a slow cooker to keep hot.

Holiday Punch

Makes 20 (8-ounce) servings

4 C. cranberry juice cocktail
8 C. lemonade
2 C. orange juice

1-4 oz. jar maraschino
   cherries
1-2 liter bottle ginger ale
1 orange, sliced in rounds

In a large punch bowl, combine cranberry juice cocktail, lemonade and orange juice. Refrigerate for 2 hours or more. When ready to serve, pour in the ginger ale. Garnish each glass with an orange slice or add orange slices to punch bowl.

Luscious Slush Punch

Makes 25 (8-ounce) servings

2 1/2 C. sugar
6 C. water
2-3 oz. pkgs. strawberry
    gelatin mix
1-46 oz. can pineapple juice

2/3 C. lemon juice
1 qt. orange juice
2-2 liter bottles lemon-
    lime soda

In a large saucepan, combine sugar, water and strawberry gelatin. Boil for 3 minutes. Stir in pineapple juice, lemon juice and orange juice. Divide mixture in half and freeze in 2 separate containers. When ready to serve, place the frozen contents of one container in a punch bowl and stir in 1 bottle of lemon-lime soda until slushy.

To choose a fresh tree, check that needles will bend, not break when pinched and bounce the tree on its trunk to be sure there isn't a shower of needles.

Apple Orchard Punch

Makes 10 (8-ounce) servings

1-32 oz. bottle apple juice, chilled
1-12 oz. can frozen cranberry juice concentrate

1 C. orange juice
1 1/2 liters ginger ale
1 apple

In a large punch bowl, combine apple juice, cranberry juice concentrate and orange juice. Stir until dissolved, then slowly pour in the ginger ale. Thinly slice the apple vertically, forming whole apple slices. Float apple slices on top of punch.

Santa's Favorite

Snacks

Party Cheese Wreath

Makes 1 wreath

2-8 oz. pkgs. cream cheese, softened
1-8 oz. pkg. shredded sharp Cheddar cheese
1 T. finely chopped onion

1 T. chopped red bell pepper
2 tsp. Worcestershire sauce
1 tsp. lemon juice
Dash ground red pepper

In a small bowl, beat the cream cheese and Cheddar cheese with an electric mixer on medium speed until well blended. Add remaining ingredients; mix well. Cover and refrigerate for several hours or overnight. Place a drinking glass in the center of a serving plate. Drop spoonfuls of cheese mixture around glass, touching outer edge of glass to form a ring. Smooth cheese with a spatula. Remove glass. If desired, garnish the top of the wreath with chopped fresh parsley and additional diced red bell pepper. Serve with crackers.

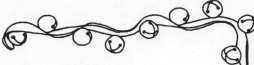

Chocolate Chip Cheese Ball

Makes 1 cheese ball

1-8 oz. pkg. cream cheese,
   softened
1/2 C. butter, softened
1 C. confectioners' sugar
2 T. brown sugar

1/4 tsp. vanilla extract
3/4 C. miniature semisweet
   chocolate chips
3/4 C. finely chopped pecans

In a medium bowl, beat together cream cheese and butter until smooth. Mix in confectioners' sugar, brown sugar and vanilla. Stir in chocolate chips. Cover and chill in the refrigerator for 2 hours. Shape chilled cream cheese mixture into a ball. Wrap with plastic and chill in the refrigerator for 1 hour. Roll the cheese ball in finely chopped pecans before serving. Serve with graham crackers or chocolate wafers.

For a quick centerpiece, fill a glass bowl or vase with round, shiny ornaments.

Cheese Ball

Makes 1 cheese ball

2-8 oz. pkgs. cream cheese,
 softened
3 1/2 C. shredded sharp
Cheddar cheese

1-1 oz. pkg. Ranch style
 dressing mix
2 C. chopped pecans
4 pecan halves

In a large bowl, mix together cream cheese, Cheddar cheese and dressing mix. Form into a ball. Roll ball in chopped pecans to coat surface. Decorate the top with pecan halves. Refrigerate for at least 2 hours or overnight.

Candy Coated Pecans

Makes 4 cups

1 egg white
1/2 C. packed brown sugar

1 dash vanilla extract
4 C. pecans

Preheat oven to 275°. Line a cookie sheet with wax paper. Spray the wax paper with cooking spray. Beat egg white until stiff. Add brown sugar and vanilla. Stir until smooth. Mix in pecans and stir until nuts are well coated. Pour the nuts onto the prepared cookie sheet. Bake until browned, approximately 10 to 15 minutes.

Candied Walnuts

Makes 1 pound

1 lb. walnut halves	**1/4 tsp. salt**
1 C. sugar	**6 T. milk**
2 tsp. ground cinnamon	**1 tsp. vanilla extract**

Preheat oven to 350°. Spread nuts in a single layer over a baking sheet. Roast for approximately 8 to 10 minutes, or until the nuts start to turn brown and the smell of roasting nuts fills the kitchen. Stir together sugar, cinnamon, salt and milk in a medium saucepan. Cook over medium-high heat for 8 minutes or until the mixture reaches the soft ball stage of 236°. Remove from heat and stir in vanilla extract immediately. Add walnuts to sugar syrup, and stir until nuts are well coated. Spoon walnuts onto wax paper and immediately separate nuts with a fork. Cool and store in airtight containers.

Cinnamon-Roasted Almonds

Makes 4 cups

1 egg white	**1/2 C. sugar**
1 tsp. cold water	**1/4 tsp. salt**
4 C. whole almonds	**1/2 tsp. ground cinnamon**

Preheat oven to 250°. Lightly grease a 10x15" jelly roll pan. Lightly beat the egg white; add water and beat until frothy but not stiff. Add the almonds and stir until well coated. Mix the sugar, salt and cinnamon then sprinkle over the nuts. Toss to coat and spread evenly on the prepared pan. Bake for 1 hour in the preheated oven, stirring occasionally, until golden. Allow almonds to cool, then store in airtight containers.

Frosted Pecan Bites

Makes 1 pound

2 egg whites	1/2 tsp. vanilla extract
1 C. sugar	1 lb. pecan halves
1 pinch salt	1/2 C. butter

Preheat oven to 325°. Beat egg whites until soft peaks begin to form. Add sugar, salt and vanilla; beat until stiff peaks form and turn glossy. Fold in pecans until well coated with the egg white mixture. Melt butter in a 9x13" baking pan by placing pan in oven. Evenly spread coated nuts over melted butter in pan. Bake for 30 minutes, stirring and turning pecans every 8 minutes or until butter no longer remains in pan. Place hot nuts on foil and allow to cool. Stored in airtight containers. Will store for several weeks.

Christmas Snack Mix

Makes 3 pounds

1-16 oz. jar dry roasted peanuts
1-14 oz. pkg. chocolate
    covered peanuts

2-14 oz. pkgs. M&M's
1-7 oz. jar wheat germ
    nuts

Mix together the peanuts, M&M's, chocolate covered peanuts and wheat germ nut snacks. Serve mixture in a large glass bowl or store in airtight containers.

Hang your Christmas cards in the shape of a tree on a wall or bulletin board.

Puppy Chow

Makes 36 servings

9 C. crispy rice cereal squares　　**1 1/2 C. confectioners'**
1/2 C. peanut butter　　　　　　　**sugar**
1 C. semisweet chocolate chips

In a saucepan over low heat, melt the chocolate. Add peanut butter and mix until smooth. Remove from heat, add cereal and stir until coated. Pour confectioners' sugar into a large plastic or paper bag, add chocolate coated cereal and shake until well coated with confectioners' sugar. Store in airtight containers.

White Chocolate Holiday Mix

Makes 4 pounds

2 lbs. white chocolate
6 C. crispy rice cereal squares
3 C. toasted oat cereal

2 C. thin pretzel sticks
2 C. cashews
1-12 oz. pkg. mini M&M's

Melt white chocolate in a large saucepan over low heat just until soft. Stir until melted. Combine crispy rice cereal squares, toasted oat cereal, pretzels, cashews and mini M&M's in a big roaster pan or bowl. Stir chocolate into mixture. Turn mixture out onto wax paper to cool. Anything you like can be added or substituted in this mix. Store in airtight containers.

Sweet Party Mix

Makes 12 cups

1-12 oz. pkg. crispy corn and rice cereal squares
5 oz. slivered almonds
6 oz. pecans, chopped and toasted

3/4 C. butter
3/4 C. dark corn syrup
1 1/2 C. brown sugar

Preheat oven to 250°. Lightly grease a large roasting pan. In a large bowl, mix crispy corn and rice cereal, slivered almonds and toasted, chopped pecans. In a medium saucepan over medium heat, melt the butter. Stir in dark corn syrup and brown sugar until well mixed. Pour the mixture over the crispy corn and rice cereal mixture. Stir and shake to coat all the nuts and cereal. Pour the coated mixture into the prepared roasting pan. Cook for 1 hour in the preheated oven, stirring approximately every 15 minutes. Cool mix on wax paper and store in airtight containers.

Best Ever Popcorn Balls

Makes 20 servings

5 qts. popped popcorn
3/4 C. light corn syrup
1/4 C. margarine

2 tsp. cold water
2 1/2 C. plus 2 T.
    confectioners' sugar
1 C. marshmallows

In a saucepan over medium heat, combine the corn syrup, margarine, cold water, confectioners' sugar and marshmallows. Heat and continually stir until the mixture comes to a boil. In a large bowl or roasting pan, carefully combine the hot syrup mixture with the popcorn, coating each kernel. Grease hands with vegetable shortening and quickly shape the coated popcorn into balls. Wrap each ball in plastic wrap to store.

Caramel Corn

Makes 8 cups

1 bag microwave popcorn
3/4 C. packed brown sugar
6 T. butter
3 T. light corn syrup

1/4 tsp. salt
1/4 tsp. baking soda
1/4 tsp. vanilla extract

Preheat oven to 300°. Pop popcorn according to package instructions. Place popcorn in a large baking pan and keep warm in the preheated oven. Discard unpopped kernels. Mix brown sugar, butter, corn syrup and salt into a large saucepan. Cook over medium heat, stirring until mixture starts to boil. Continue cooking for 5 minutes without stirring. Remove from heat. Stir in baking soda and vanilla. Pour over the popped popcorn. Bake for 25 to 30 minutes in the preheated oven, stirring every 10 minutes. Remove from pan and put into a large bowl to cool. Store in an airtight container.

Santa's Favorite

Breads

Pumpkin Cheese Bread

Makes 2 (8 1/2x4") loaves

1-8 oz. pkg. cream cheese
1/2 C. sugar
1 T. flour
1 egg
1 T. orange zest
1 2/3 C. flour
1 tsp. baking soda
1/2 tsp. salt

1/2 tsp. ground cinnamon
1/2 tsp. ground cloves
    cinnamon
1/2 tsp. pumpkin pie
    spice
1 C. pumpkin puree
1/2 C. vegetable oil
2 eggs
1 1/2 C. sugar

Preheat oven to 325°. Lightly grease two 8 1/2x4" loaf pans. In a medium bowl, combine cream cheese, 1/2 cup sugar, 1 tablespoon flour, 1 egg and orange zest; beat until smooth. Set mixture aside. Sift together 1 2/3 cups flour, baking soda, salt, cinnamon, cloves and pumpkin pie spice; set aside. Place pumpkin, oil, 2 eggs and 1 1/2 cups sugar in a large bowl and beat well. Stir the pumpkin mixture into the flour mixture just until combined. Pour 1/2 of the pumpkin batter into the loaf pans. Spoon cream cheese mixture on top of this layer and then pour on the remaining batter. Bake in preheated oven for 60 to 70 minutes or until a toothpick inserted into the center of the loaf comes out clean. Cool bread in pans for 10 minutes before removing to a wire rack to cool completely.

Cherry Pecan Bread

Makes 1 (9x5") loaf

1/2 C. butter or margarine
3/4 C. sugar
2 eggs
1 tsp. baking soda
1/2 tsp. salt
1 tsp. vanilla extract

1 C. buttermilk
2 C. flour
1-10 oz. jar maraschino
    cherries, drained and
    chopped
1 C. chopped pecans

Preheat oven to 350°. Grease a 9x5" loaf pan. In a large bowl, cream butter and sugar together. Add eggs and continue mixing until light and fluffy. Add baking soda, salt and vanilla; mix thoroughly. Alternately add buttermilk and flour to the creamed mixture, mixing only enough to hold ingredients together. Fold in cherries and nuts. Turn batter into prepared pan. Bake for 50 to 60 minutes or until bread tests done. Cool completely before slicing. If desired, top with a powdered sugar glaze.

Keep a scrapbook to fill with your favorite Christmas cards and letters each year.

Cinnamon Bread

Makes 1 (9x5") loaf

2 C. flour
1 C. sugar
2 tsp. baking powder
1/2 tsp. baking soda
1 1/2 tsp. ground cinnamon
1 tsp. salt
1 C. buttermilk

1/4 C. vegetable oil
2 eggs
2 tsp. vanilla extract
2 T. sugar
1 tsp. ground cinnamon
2 tsp. butter or margarine

Preheat oven to 350°. Grease a 9x5" loaf pan. Measure flour, 1 cup sugar, baking powder, baking soda, 1 1/2 teaspoons cinnamon, salt, buttermilk, oil, eggs and vanilla into large mixing bowl. Beat for 3 minutes. Pour batter into prepared loaf pan. Smooth the top of the batter. Combine 2 tablespoons sugar, 1 teaspoon cinnamon and butter, mixing until crumbly. Sprinkle topping over smoothed batter. Using a knife, cut a light swirling motion into the batter to give it a marbled effect. Bake for approximately 50 minutes or until a toothpick inserted into the center comes out clean. Remove bread from pan to a wire rack to cool.

Sweet Potato Bread

Makes 1 (8 1/2x4") loaf

1 1/2 C. flour
2 tsp. baking powder
1/4 tsp. salt
1 tsp. ground nutmeg
1/2 tsp. ground cinnamon
1 C. sugar
2 eggs, beaten

1/2 C. vegetable oil
2 T. milk
1 C. cooked and mashed
    sweet potatoes
1 C. chopped pecans
1/2 C. golden raisins

Preheat oven to 325°. Grease an 8 1/2x4" loaf pan. In a medium bowl, stir together the flour, baking powder, salt, nutmeg, cinnamon and sugar. Add the eggs, oil and milk; mix until well blended. Finally, stir in the mashed sweet potatoes, pecans and golden raisins. Pour the batter into the prepared pan and bake for 70 minutes or until a toothpick inserted in the center comes out clean. Allow bread to cool in the pan for at least 15 minutes before removing. For best flavor, store overnight before serving.

Pumpkin Gingerbread

Makes 2 (9x5") loaves

3 C. sugar
1 C. vegetable oil
4 eggs
2/3 C. water
1-15 oz. can pumpkin puree
2 tsp. ground ginger
1 tsp. ground allspice

1 tsp. ground cinnamon
1 tsp. ground cloves
3 1/2 C. flour
2 tsp. baking soda
1 1/2 tsp. salt
1/2 tsp. baking powder

Preheat oven to 350°. Lightly grease two 9x5" loaf pans. In a large mixing bowl, combine sugar, oil and eggs; beat until smooth. Add water and beat until well blended. Stir in pumpkin, ginger, allspice, cinnamon and cloves. In a medium bowl, combine flour, baking soda, salt and baking powder. Add dry ingredients to pumpkin mixture and blend just until all ingredients are mixed. Divide batter between prepared pans. Bake in preheated oven for approximately 1 hour or until a toothpick inserted into the center comes out clean.

Plum Bread

Makes 1 (9x5") loaf or 1 bundt cake

1 C. vegetable oil
3 eggs
2-4 oz. jars plum baby food
2 C. sugar
1 tsp. red food coloring
2 C. flour
1 tsp. ground cloves

1 tsp. ground cinnamon
1/2 tsp. ground nutmeg
1/2 tsp. salt
1/2 tsp. baking soda
1 C. chopped nuts
1 C. confectioners' sugar
2 1/2 T. lemon juice

Preheat oven to 350°. In a large bowl, mix oil, eggs, baby food, sugar and food coloring. In a separate bowl, mix together flour, cloves, cinnamon, nutmeg, salt, baking soda and nuts. Mix wet and dry ingredients together until just combined. Place batter into a greased and floured bundt pan or 9x5" loaf pan. Bake for 50 to 60 minutes or until it tests done. Remove from oven to cool 10 minutes in pan. Remove bread from pan and place on cooling rack. While cooling, combine confectioners' sugar and lemon juice. Brush over top while bread is still hot.

Cranberry Nut Bread

Makes 1 (9x5") loaf

2 C. flour
3/4 C. sugar
3/4 tsp. salt
1 1/2 tsp. baking powder
1/2 tsp. baking soda
1 C. chopped cranberries

1/2 C. chopped nuts
1 T. orange zest
1 egg
2 T. vegetable oil
3/4 C. orange juice

Preheat oven to 350°. Grease a 9x5" loaf pan. In a large bowl, combine flour, sugar, salt, baking powder and baking soda. Add the cranberries and chopped nuts and stir to coat with flour. Combine the orange zest, egg, oil and orange juice. Add the egg mixture to the flour mixture and stir until just combined. Spoon the batter into the prepared pan. Bake for 50 minutes or until a toothpick inserted in the center comes out clean. Let bread sit for 10 minutes and then remove from the pan and place on a wire cooling rack. Let bread cool completely before slicing.

Chocolate Chip Pumpkin Bread

Makes 3 (9x5") loaves

3 C. sugar
1-15 oz. can pumpkin puree
1 C. vegetable oil
2/3 C. water
4 eggs
3 1/2 C. flour
1 T. ground cinnamon

1 T. ground nutmeg
2 tsp. baking soda
1 1/2 tsp. salt
1 C. miniature semisweet
   chocolate chips
1/2 C. chopped walnuts,
   optional

Preheat oven to 350°. Grease and flour three 9x5" loaf pans. In a large bowl, combine sugar, pumpkin, oil, water and eggs. Beat until smooth. Blend in flour, cinnamon, nutmeg, baking soda and salt. Fold in chocolate chips and, if desired, walnuts. Place batter in prepared loaf pans. Bake for 1 hour or until a toothpick inserted in the center comes out clean. Cool on wire racks before removing from pans.

To remove dust from Christmas decorations, blow air on them using a blow dryer on the lowest setting.

Eggnog Quick Bread

Makes 1 (9x5") loaf

2 eggs, beaten
1 C. eggnog
2 tsp. rum flavored extract
1 C. sugar
1 tsp. vanilla extract

1/2 C. butter, softened
2 1/4 C. flour
2 tsp. baking powder
1/2 tsp. salt
1/4 tsp. ground nutmeg

Preheat oven to 350°. Grease only the bottom of a 9x5" loaf pan. Blend together the eggs, eggnog, rum extract, sugar, vanilla and butter. Sift together the flour, baking powder, salt and nutmeg. Add to the eggnog mixture and stir just enough to moisten; pour batter into prepared pan. Bake bread for 40 to 60 minutes or until a toothpick inserted in the center comes out clean. Cool for 10 minutes and remove from pan. Cool completely, wrap tightly and store in refrigerator.

Cranberry Orange Loaf

Makes 1 (9x5") loaf

2 C. flour
1 1/2 tsp. baking powder
1/2 tsp. baking soda
1/2 tsp. salt
1 T. orange zest
1 1/2 C. fresh cranberries

1/2 C. pecans, coarsely
    chopped
1/4 C. margarine,
    softened
1 C. sugar
1 egg
3/4 C. orange juice

Preheat oven to 350°. Grease and flour a 9x5" loaf pan. Whisk together flour, baking powder, baking soda and salt. Stir in orange zest, cranberries and pecans. Set aside. In a large bowl, cream margarine, sugar and egg until smooth. Stir in orange juice. Beat in flour mixture until just moistened. Pour batter into prepared pan. Bake for 1 hour in the preheated oven or until the bread springs back when lightly touched. Let stand 10 minutes, then turn out onto a wire rack to cool.

Pumpkin Bread

Makes 3 (7x3") loaves

1-15 oz. can pumpkin puree
4 eggs
1 C. vegetable oil
2/3 C. water
3 C. sugar
3 1/2 C. flour

2 tsp. baking soda
1 1/2 tsp. salt
1 tsp. ground cinnamon
1 tsp. ground nutmeg
1/2 tsp. ground cloves
1/4 tsp. ground ginger

Preheat oven to 350°. Grease and flour three 7x3" loaf pans. In a large bowl, mix together pumpkin, eggs, oil, water and sugar until well blended. In a separate bowl, whisk together the flour, baking soda, salt, cinnamon, nutmeg, cloves and ginger. Stir the dry ingredients into the pumpkin mixture until just combined. Pour batter into the prepared pans. Bake for approximately 50 minutes in the preheated oven or until a toothpick inserted in the center comes out clean.

Cinnamon Applesauce Bread

Makes 1 (9x5") loaf pan

1 1/2 C. flour
1 T. baking powder
1 1/2 tsp. ground cinnamon
1/4 tsp. salt
1 egg
1 C. chunky applesauce

3/4 C. firmly packed
  brown sugar
2/3 C. skim milk
2 T. vegetable oil
1 1/2 C. bran flakes cereal
1/4 C. chopped walnuts,
  optional

Preheat oven to 350°. Grease a 9x5" loaf pan. In a large bowl, combine flour, baking powder, cinnamon and salt. In a separate bowl, beat egg then stir in applesauce, brown sugar, milk and oil. Add to flour mixture and stir just until moistened. Batter will be lumpy. Stir in cereal and, if desired, walnuts. Pour batter into prepared pan. Bake for 55 minutes or until a toothpick inserted in the center comes out clean.

Old Fashioned Gingerbread

Makes 1 (9") square cake

1/2 C. sugar
1/2 C. butter, softened
1 egg
1 C. molasses
2 1/2 C. flour
1 1/2 tsp. baking soda

1 tsp. ground cinnamon
1 tsp. ground ginger
1/2 tsp. ground cloves
1/2 tsp. salt
1 C. hot water

Preheat oven to 350°. Grease and flour a 9" square pan. In a large bowl, cream together the sugar and butter. Beat in egg then mix in the molasses. In a separate bowl, sift together flour, baking soda, cinnamon, ginger, cloves and salt. Blend into the creamed mixture. Stir in the hot water. Pour batter into the prepared pan. Bake for 1 hour or until a toothpick inserted in the center comes out clean. Allow to cool in pan before serving.

Orange Pumpkin Loaf

Makes 1 (9x5") loaf

1 large orange	1 tsp. baking soda
1/3 C. butter, softened	1/2 tsp. baking powder
1 1/3 C. sugar	3/4 tsp. salt
2 eggs	1/2 tsp. ground cinnamon
1 C. canned pumpkin	1/2 tsp. ground cloves
1/3 C. water	1/2 C. chopped walnuts
2 C. flour	1/2 C. chopped raisins

Preheat oven to 350°. Grease a 9x5" loaf pan. Cut orange into wedges and remove seeds. Place orange, peel and all, in a food processor. Pulse until finely chopped then set aside. In a large bowl, cream butter and sugar until smooth. Beat in eggs one at a time, then stir in pumpkin, water and the ground orange. In a separate bowl, mix together flour, baking soda, baking powder, salt, cinnamon and cloves. Stir into batter just until moistened. Fold in nuts and raisins. Spoon batter into prepared pan. Bake for 1 hour or until a toothpick inserted in the center comes out clean. Let bread stand for 10 minutes, then remove from pan and cool on a wire rack.

Keep your tablecloths wrinkle free by storing them in empty wrapping paper rolls.

Banana Sour Cream Bread

Makes 4 (7x3") loaves

1/4 C. sugar
1 tsp. ground cinnamon
3/4 C. butter, softened
3 C. sugar
3 eggs
6 very ripe bananas, mashed
1-16 oz. tub sour cream

2 tsp. vanilla extract
2 tsp. ground cinnamon
1/2 tsp. salt
3 tsp. baking soda
4 1/2 C. flour
1 C. chopped walnuts,
    optional

Preheat oven to 300°. Grease four 7x3" loaf pans. In a small bowl, stir together 1/4 cup sugar and 1 teaspoon cinnamon. Dust pans lightly with cinnamon and sugar mixture. In a large bowl, cream butter and 3 cups sugar. Mix in eggs, mashed bananas, sour cream, vanilla and 2 teaspoons cinnamon. Stir in salt, baking soda and flour. If desired, fold in walnuts. Divide batter into prepared pans. Bake for 1 hour or until a toothpick inserted in the center comes out clean.

Santa's Favorite
Candy

Candy Making Tips

Flawless Fudge

While these tips seem simple enough, they are truly vital to creating a good batch of fudge.

It is extremely important to follow the recipe's directions very carefully. Substituting ingredients, adding ingredients out of order or skipping a step can be disastrous when making fudge. Be sure to stir when the directions tell you to stir and don't stir when the recipe tells you not to.

For the best results, use a large, heavy saucepan that holds about twice the volume of your recipe. Finally, before you start the process of making fudge, be prepared. Once you start making fudge, you can't stop without the risk ruining the batch. Have all of the necessary tools within reach, your pans greased or lined and the ingredients measured.

Dandy Candy

Before you begin, you must take the weather into account. On humid (higher than 60%) or rainy days, the cooking times can vary and because sugar attracts water causing the candy to never completely set up. A dry day is always better for candy making.

When making candy, use only the best ingredients. Start with an unopened bag of sugar to ensure that it has not been contaminated in anyway. Also, never use margarine when the recipe calls for butter and always use unsalted butter in candy recipes as the salt in salted butter can greatly affect your finished product.

If the recipe calls for you to use a candy thermometer, test the thermometer beforehand. To do this, clip the thermometer to the side of a pan of water and bring the water to a boil. Never immerse the thermometer into already boiling water as it will break your thermometer. The temperature should read 212 degrees F. To get an accurate reading when using the thermometer, the bulb should never touch the sides or the bottom of a pan.

Caramels

Makes 4 to 5 dozen

2 C. sugar
1 C. packed brown sugar
1 C. corn syrup
1 C. evaporated milk

2 C. heavy whipping
   cream
1 C. butter
1 1/4 tsp. vanilla extract

Grease a 12x15" pan. In a medium-size pot over low heat, combine sugar, brown sugar, corn syrup, evaporated milk, whipping cream and butter. Once the sugar has dissolved into the liquids, bring to a boil, constantly stirring. Monitor the heat of the mixture with a candy thermometer while stirring. When the thermometer reaches 250°, remove the pot from the heat. Stir in vanilla. Transfer mixture to the prepared pan and let the mixture cool completely. When cooled, cut the caramel into small squares and wrap them in wax paper for storage.

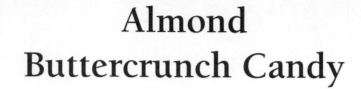

Almond Buttercrunch Candy

Makes 3 1/2 pounds

2-11.5 oz. pkgs. milk chocolate chips, divided
2 C. butter

1 lb. brown sugar
1 C. blanched slivered almonds, divided

Preheat oven to 200°. Grease a 14x17 1/2" cookie sheet with sides. Sprinkle one package of chocolate chips on prepared pan. Place in warm oven until chips melt, about 5 minutes. Remove from oven and spread melted chocolate over bottom of pan; set aside. In a large heavy saucepan over medium-high heat, combine butter and brown sugar. Stirring constantly, heat to 300 to 310° or until a small amount of syrup dropped into cold water forms hard, brittle threads. Immediately remove from heat. Stir in 3/4 cup slivered almonds and pour into pan with melted chocolate; spread mixture evenly over chocolate. Sprinkle remaining package of chocolate chips over the almond layer. The heat from the almond layer will melt the chocolate chips; spread melted chocolate evenly. Sprinkle remaining 1/4 cup almonds over chocolate. Cut into squares or allow to harden in a solid sheet and break it apart like brittle. Cool completely before removing from pan.

Divinity

Makes 1 1/2 dozen

2 C. sugar	**1/4 tsp. salt**
1/2 C. light corn syrup	**2 egg whites**
1/2 C. hot water	**1 tsp. vanilla extract**

In a heavy, 2-quart saucepan, combine the sugar, corn syrup, hot water and salt. Cook, stirring constantly, until the sugar dissolves and the mixture comes to a boil. Then cook without stirring to 250°. Frequently wipe crystals forming on the sides of the pan, using a pastry brush dipped in water. Remove from heat. Just as the syrup is reaching temperature, begin whipping egg whites in a large glass or stainless steel mixing bowl. Beat egg whites until stiff peaks form. Pour hot mixture in a thin stream over beaten egg whites, beating constantly with the electric mixer at medium speed. Increase speed to high and continue beating for about 5 minutes. Add vanilla; continue beating until the mixture becomes stiff and begins to lose its gloss. If it is too stiff, add a few drops of hot water. Immediately drop by teaspoonfuls onto wax paper. For a decorative flair, swirl the top with the spoon when dropping. Let stand until set. Store in an airtight container at room temperature.

Hard Rock Candy

Makes 3 pounds

1 C. confectioners' sugar
3 3/4 C. sugar
1 1/2 C. light corn syrup

1 C. water
2 tsp. cinnamon oil
1 tsp. red food coloring

Roll the edges of two 16" square pieces of heavy-duty aluminum foil. Sprinkle the foil very generously with confectioners' sugar. In a large, heavy saucepan, combine the sugar, corn syrup and water. Heat over medium-high heat, stirring constantly until sugar dissolves. Stop stirring and boil to 300 to 310°. Remove from heat. Stir in the cinnamon oil and food coloring. Pour onto the prepared foil and allow to cool and harden. Crack into pieces and store in an airtight container. Flavors and coloring can be varied by substituting lemon, orange, peppermint and other oils and food coloring.

Chocolate Caramels

Makes 4 dozen

1 1/2 C. light cream
1 C. sugar
3/4 C. light corn syrup

3 squares semisweet
    baking chocolate
1/4 tsp. salt

Mix all ingredients in medium saucepan. Bring to boil over low heat, stirring constantly. Cook, stirring constantly, until mixture is thickened and reaches 246°. Pour into lightly buttered 8x4" loaf pan. Do not scrape saucepan. Let mixture stand until set. Score candy into 3/4" squares with a sharp knife. Invert candy onto a cool surface then turn over so marked side is up. Cut candy into squares, using full length of long sharp blade of knife. Wrap each caramel in wax paper for storage. Let stand in cool place overnight to set. Store at room temperature.

For gift giving, put homemade candies in mini cupcake liners and place them in a small shallow box.

Almond Crunch

Makes 2 pounds

1 C. blanched slivered almonds **2 T. light corn syrup**
1 C. butter **2 T. water**
1 1/4 C. sugar **2 C. milk chocolate chips**

Preheat oven to 375°. Arrange almonds in a single layer on a baking sheet. Toast almonds in the preheated oven for approximately 5 minutes or until lightly browned. Line a jelly roll pan with foil. In a heavy saucepan, combine butter, sugar, corn syrup and water. Cook over medium heat, stirring constantly, until mixture boils. Boil, without stirring, to 300°. Remove from heat. Working quickly, stir in almonds and pour mixture into foil-lined jelly roll pan; tip pan from side to side to spread candy evenly in pan. Sprinkle chocolate chips over candy brittle. Let stand about 5 minutes or until chocolate is shiny and soft. Spread chocolate evenly over candy. Cool to room temperature, then refrigerate for 1 hour. Break into bite-size pieces.

Melt In Your Mouth Toffee

Makes 48 servings

1 lb. butter
1 C. sugar
1 C. packed brown sugar

1 C. chopped walnuts
2 C. semisweet chocolate chips

In a heavy saucepan, combine butter, sugar and brown sugar. Cook over medium heat, stirring constantly, until mixture boils. Boil to 300° without stirring. Remove from heat. Pour nuts and chocolate chips into a 9x13" dish. Pour hot mixture over the nuts and chocolate. Use a lightly oiled spoon to spread mixture evenly. Let the mixture cool and break it into pieces for serving.

Creamy Chocolate Fudge

Makes 3 pounds

1-7 oz. jar marshmallow crème
1 1/2 C. sugar
2/3 C. evaporated milk
1/4 C. butter
1/4 tsp. salt

2 C. milk chocolate chips
1 C. semisweet chocolate chips
1/2 C. chopped nuts
1 tsp. vanilla extract

Line an 8x8" pan with foil or wax paper. Set aside. In a large saucepan over medium heat, combine marshmallow crème, sugar, evaporated milk, butter and salt until sugar is dissolved. Then bring to a full boil and cook for 5 minutes, stirring constantly. Remove from heat and pour in chocolate chips and milk chocolate chips. Stir until chocolate is melted and mixture is smooth. Stir in nuts and vanilla. Pour mixture into prepared pan. Chill in refrigerator for 2 hours or until firm. Cut fudge into small squares and wrap individually with wax paper for storage.

Raspberry Truffle Fudge

Makes 2 1/2 pounds

3 C. semisweet chocolate
  chips
1-14 oz. can sweetened
  condensed milk
1 1/2 tsp. vanilla extract

Salt to taste
1/4 C. heavy cream
1/4 C. raspberry jam,
  melted
2 C. semisweet chocolate
  chips

Spray a 9x9" pan with non-stick cooking spray and line with foil or wax paper. In a microwave-safe bowl, combine 3 cups chocolate chips and sweetened condensed milk. Heat in microwave until chocolate melts, stirring often until smooth. Be careful not to let it scorch. Stir in the vanilla and salt. Spread chocolate mixture into prepared pan and cool to room temperature. In a microwave-safe bowl, combine cream, melted raspberry jam and 2 cups chocolate chips. Heat in microwave until chocolate melts, stirring often until smooth. Cool mixture to lukewarm, then pour over the fudge layer. Refrigerate until both layers are completely set, about 1 hour. Cut into 1" pieces.

White Chocolate Fudge

Makes 2 1/2 pounds

1-8 oz. pkg. cream cheese
4 C. confectioners' sugar
1 1/2 tsp. vanilla extract

12 oz. white chocolate,
chopped
3/4 C. chopped pecans

Grease an 8" square baking dish. Set aside. In a medium bowl, beat cream cheese, sugar and vanilla until smooth. In the top of a double boiler over lightly simmering water, heat white chocolate, stirring until melted and smooth. Fold melted white chocolate and pecans into cream cheese mixture. Spread into prepared baking dish. Chill for 1 hour, and then cut into 1" squares.

No-Cook
Never Fail Fudge

Makes 20 servings

1/2 lb. processed cheese food, cubed	2 lbs. confectioners' sugar
1/2 lb. butter	1 1/2 C. chopped walnuts or pecans
1/2 C. unsweetened cocoa powder	1 1/2 tsp. vanilla extract

Melt cheese and butter together in a non-stick saucepan; stirring often until smooth. Keep this mixture over a low heat, stirring occasionally. In a mixing bowl, sift confectioners' sugar and cocoa together until thoroughly mixed and no lumps remain. Combine the sugar mixture with the melted butter and cheese. Stir until very smooth. Stir in nuts and vanilla. Press mixture into lightly greased 9x13" pan; let cool until firm. Cut into 1" squares.

Store rolls of ribbon on an upright paper towel holder for easy access.

Double-Decker Fudge

Makes 2 pounds

1 C. peanut butter chips   3/4 C. evaporated milk
1 C. semisweet chocolate chips 1/4 C. butter
2 1/4 C. sugar   1 tsp. vanilla extract
1-7 oz. jar marshmallow crème

Line 8" square pan with foil or wax paper extending foil over edges of pan. Measure peanut butter chips into one medium bowl and chocolate chips into second medium bowl. Combine sugar, marshmallow crème, evaporated milk and butter in heavy 3-quart saucepan. Cook over medium heat, stirring constantly, until mixture boils. Boil and stir for 5 minutes. Remove from heat and stir in vanilla. Immediately stir half of the hot mixture (1 1/2 cups) into peanut butter chips until chips are completely melted; quickly pour into prepared pan. Stir remaining half of the hot mixture into chocolate chips until chips are completely melted. Quickly spread over top of peanut butter layer. Cool completely. Remove from pan; place on cutting board. Peel off and discard foil; cut into 1" squares.

Easy Peanut Butter Fudge

Makes 15 servings

1/2 C. butter
2 C. packed brown sugar
1/2 C. milk

1 C. peanut butter
1 tsp. vanilla extract
3 C. confectioners' sugar

Melt butter in a medium saucepan over medium heat. Stir in brown sugar and milk. Bring to a boil and boil for 2 minutes, stirring constantly. Remove from heat. Stir in peanut butter and vanilla. Pour mixture over confectioners' sugar in a large mixing bowl. Beat until smooth. Pour into an 8" square pan lined with foil or wax paper. Chill until firm, lift out and cut into 1" squares.

Quick & Easy Fudge

Makes 12 servings

4 C. confectioners' sugar	1/4 C. milk
1/2 C. unsweetened cocoa powder	1/2 C. butter
	2 tsp. vanilla extract

Grease a 9" square pan or line with foil or wax paper. In a microwave safe bowl, stir together confectioners' sugar and cocoa. Pour milk over mixture and place butter in bowl. Do not mix. Microwave until butter is melted, approximately 2 minutes. Stir in vanilla and stir vigorously until smooth. Pour into prepared dish. Chill in freezer for 10 minutes before cutting into 1" squares.

Before burning candles, lightly coat candlesticks with vegetable spray. Any wax that drips onto the candlesticks can easily be removed.

Chocolate Covered Peppermint Patties

Makes 4 dozen

1 C. mashed potatoes
1 tsp. salt
2 T. melted butter
2 tsp. peppermint extract

6-8 C. confectioners' sugar
8-1 oz. squares semisweet
chocolate
2 T. shortening

In a large bowl, mix together the potatoes, salt, butter and peppermint extract. Gradually mix in 6 to 8 cups confectioners' sugar, enough to make a workable dough. Knead slightly and roll into cherry-size balls. Flatten balls to form patties. Arrange on sheets of wax paper and allow to dry overnight. Place chocolate and shortening in a microwave-safe bowl. Heat in microwave, stirring occasionally, until melted and smooth. Dip patties in melted chocolate and let cool on wax paper.

Easy Pralines

Makes 3 dozen

1 lb. light brown sugar
1 C. heavy whipping cream
2 T. light corn syrup

1 T. butter
2 C. chopped toasted
** pecans**

In a deep, microwave-safe bowl, mix together brown sugar, whipping cream and corn syrup. Microwave on high for 13 minutes. Mix in butter until well blended. Then stir, stir and stir some more until mixture begins to cool and get creamy. Stir in chopped pecans. Drop candy by tablespoonfuls onto wax paper to cool.

Coconut-Almond Balls

Makes 26 servings

4 C. flaked coconut
1/4 C. light corn syrup
1-12 oz. pkg. semisweet
    chocolate chips

1/4 C. shortening
26 whole almonds

Line two cookie sheets or a large flat surface with wax paper and place large cooling rack on top of the wax paper. Place coconut in a large bowl. Heat corn syrup in microwave for approximately 1 minute until syrup boils. Pour syrup immediately over coconut and stir until well mixed. Using a tablespoon measure, shape coconut mixture into 26 balls with hands and place on wire racks. Let rest for 10 minutes, then re-roll each ball to keep loose ends from sticking out. Heat shortening and chocolate together in a large glass bowl in microwave, or in saucepan on stove top, stirring frequently until chocolate is melted and smooth. Working quickly, spoon 1 tablespoon of chocolate over each ball. Lightly press an almond on top of each ball. Let balls stand until set.

Easy Peanut Brittle

Makes 1 pound

1 1/2 C. dry roasted peanuts
1 C. sugar
1/2 C. light corn syrup
1 pinch salt, optional

1 T. butter
1 tsp. vanilla extract
1 tsp. baking soda

Grease a baking sheet and set aside. In a glass bowl, combine peanuts, sugar, corn syrup and salt until well mixed. Heat in microwave for 6 or 7 minutes on high until mixture is bubbly and peanuts are browned. Stir in butter and vanilla; cook for 2 to 3 minutes longer. Quickly stir in baking soda, just until mixture is foamy. Pour immediately onto greased baking sheet. Let cool for 15 minutes or until set. Break into pieces and store in an airtight container.

Cherry Cookie Balls

Makes 4 dozen

1 C. semisweet chocolate
  chips
2 to 4 T. rum extract, optional
1/4 C. light corn syrup
3 C. fine vanilla water crumbs
  (about 80 cookies)

1 1/2 C. finely chopped
  pecans
1/2 C. confectioners' sugar
Additional confectioners'
  sugar
Red candied cherries,
  halved (optional)

Place chocolate chips in small microwave-safe bowl. Microwave at high for 1 minute, stirring frequently until chips are melted and smooth. Stir in rum extract and corn syrup. Stir together vanilla wafer crumbs, pecans and 1/2 cup confectioners' sugar. Drizzle chocolate mixture over crumb mixture, stirring until blended. Shape mixture into 1" balls; roll in confectioners' sugar. If desired, place cherry half in center of each cookie, pressing down lightly.

Avoid struggling while hanging outdoor Christmas lights by screwing small hooks around door and window frames to hang the lights from. Leave the hooks up all year making decorating faster each year after.

Chocolate Cashew Macadamia Crunch

Makes 1/2 pound

2 C. milk chocolate chips
3/4 C. coarsely chopped salted
    or unsalted cashews
3/4 C. coarsely chopped salted
    or unsalted macadamia nuts

1/2 C. butter, softened
1/2 C. sugar
2 T. light corn syrup

Line a 9" square pan with foil, extending foil over edges of pan; butter foil. Cover bottom of prepared pan with chocolate chips. Combine cashews, macadamia nuts, butter, sugar and corn syrup in large heavy skillet. Cook over low heat, stirring constantly, until butter is melted and sugar is dissolved. Increase heat to medium, stirring constantly until mixture begins to cling together and turns golden brown. Pour mixture over chocolate chips in pan, spreading evenly. Cool until chocolate is firm. Remove from pan; peel off foil. Break into pieces. Store tightly covered in cool, dry place.

Cocoa Balls

Makes 4 dozen

1-12 oz. pkg. vanilla wafers, crushed

1 1/2 C. chopped nuts

3/4 C. confectioners' sugar

1/4 C. unsweetened cocoa powder

2 to 4 T. rum extract, optional

3 T. light corn syrup

2 T. confectioners' sugar

In a large bowl, combine vanilla wafer crumbs, chopped nuts, 3/4 cup confectioners' sugar and cocoa. Mix in rum extract and corn syrup. Shape dough into 1" balls; roll in confectioners' sugar. Store cocoa balls in an airtight container.

Peppermint Meringues

Makes 4 dozen

2 egg whites
1/8 tsp. salt
1/8 tsp. cream of tartar

1/2 C. sugar
2 peppermint candy canes,
    crushed

Preheat oven to 225°. Line 2 cookie sheets with foil. In a large glass or metal mixing bowl, beat egg whites, salt and cream of tartar to soft peaks. Gradually add sugar, continuing to beat until whites form stiff peaks. Drop by spoonfuls 1" apart on the prepared cookie sheets. Sprinkle crushed peppermint candy over the cookies. Bake for 1 1/2 hours. Meringues should be completely dry on the inside. Do not allow them to brown. Turn off oven. Keep oven door ajar and let meringues sit in the oven until completely cool. Loosen from foil with metal spatula. Store loosely covered in cool dry place for up to 2 months.

Cranberry Macadamia Nut Bark

Makes 1 1/2 pounds

1 lb. almond bark
1/2 C. dried cranberries

1-3.5 oz. pkg. macadamia
nuts

Line a 15x10" cookie sheet with aluminum foil. Place almond bark in a microwave safe bowl. Heat in microwave on medium, stirring frequently, until melted and smooth. Stir in cranberries and nuts. Spread mixture out in prepared pan, cool and break into 1 1/2" pieces. Store in airtight container.

Butter Rum Brittle

Makes 12 servings

24 squares graham crackers
3-1.14 oz. rolls butter
   rum Life Savers,
   finely crushed

1 C. miniature semisweet
   chocolate chips
1/4 C. pecans, finely
   chopped and toasted

Preheat oven to 350°. Line 15x10x1" baking sheet with foil. Place graham crackers in single layer. Sprinkle crushed candy over crackers. Bake for 6 minutes or until candy is melted. Quickly sprinkle chocolate chips over melted candy. Bake an additional 2 to 3 minutes. Remove from oven and spread melted chips with spatula. Sprinkle with pecans. Cool completely; break into pieces. Store in airtight container.

Chocolate &
Peanut Butter Truffles

Makes 3 1/2 dozen

3/4 C. butter
1 C. peanut butter chips
1/2 C. unsweetened cocoa
   powder
1-14 oz. can sweetened
   condensed milk

1 T. vanilla extract
Cocoa, finely chopped nuts
   or graham
   cracker crumbs

Melt butter and peanut butter chips in a large saucepan over low heat, stirring often. Add cocoa and stir until smooth. Stir in sweetened condensed milk; stir constantly for approximately 4 minutes or until mixture is thick and glossy. Remove from heat and stir in vanilla. Refrigerate for 2 hours or until firm enough to handle. Shape into 1" balls; roll in cocoa, nuts or graham cracker crumbs. Refrigerate until firm, about 1 hour. Store, covered, in refrigerator.

Buckeye Balls

Makes 60 servings

1 1/2 C. peanut butter
1/2 C. butter, softened
1 tsp. vanilla extract
4 C. confectioners' sugar,
   sifted

6 oz. semisweet chocolate
   chips
2 T. shortening

Line a baking sheet with wax paper and set aside. In a medium bowl, mix peanut butter, butter, vanilla and confectioners' sugar with hands to form a smooth, stiff dough. Shape dough into balls using 2 teaspoons of dough for each ball. Place on a prepared pan and refrigerate. Melt shortening and chips together in a metal bowl over a pan of lightly simmering water. Stir occasionally until smooth. Remove balls from refrigerator. Insert a toothpick into a ball and dip into melted chocolate. Return ball to wax paper and remove toothpick. Repeat with remaining balls. Refrigerate for 30 minutes to set.

Macadamia Turtles

Makes 24 servings

3/4 to 1 lb. macadamia nuts
1-14 oz. pkg. caramels,
    unwrapped
3 T. heavy cream

1-11 oz. pkg. milk chocolate
    chips
1 T. shortening

Cover 2 cookie sheets with wax paper; coat wax paper with non-stick cooking spray. Arrange the macadamia nuts into 24 groups on the cookie sheets. In a small saucepan, melt the caramels with the cream over low heat for 5 to 7 minutes, or until smooth, stirring constantly. Spoon the caramel mixture over each nut group quickly while still hot (reheat if caramel gets too thick). In another small saucepan, melt the chocolate chips with the shortening over low heat for 5 to 7 minutes, or until smooth, stirring constantly. Drizzle the chocolate over the caramel and nuts and let stand until firm.

Rocky Road Drops

Makes 4 dozen

**1-12 oz. pkg. semisweet
chocolate chips**
2 C. butterscotch chips
2 C. raisins

2 C. peanuts
**2 C. miniature
marshmallows**
4 C. chow mein noodles

In the top of a double boiler, melt the chocolate and butterscotch chips. In a large bowl, combine the raisins, peanuts, marshmallows and chow mein noodles. Add melted chocolate mixture and quickly mix well. Drop by tablespoons onto wax paper; allow to sit until chocolate is set.

Peppermint Brittle

Makes 36 servings

2 lbs. white chocolate   **30 small peppermint candy canes**

Line a 15x10x1" pan with heavy-duty foil. Place candy canes in a plastic bag or between two pieces of wax paper. Using a mallet or rolling pin, break the candy canes into small chunks. Place white chocolate in a microwave-safe bowl. Heat in microwave on medium setting for 5 to 6 minutes. Stir occasionally, until chocolate is melted and smooth. Stir crushed peppermint into melted white chocolate. Spread evenly in pan and chill until set, about 1 hour. Break into pieces by slamming pan on counter.

Chocolate Crunch Buttons

Makes 2 dozen

24 circular pretzels   **24 M&M's**
24 milk chocolate candy kisses

Preheat oven to 350°. Place pretzels on baking sheets. Unwrap candy kisses and place one in the center of each pretzel. Place in preheated oven 1 to 2 minutes, until kisses melt. Remove from oven and place one M&M in the center of each pretzel. Chill in refrigerator until set.

Fudge Bonbons

Makes 60 servings

**2 C. semisweet chocolate
   chips
1/4 C. butter
1-14 oz. can sweetened
   condensed milk**

**2 C. flour
1 tsp. vanilla extract
60 milk chocolate candy
   kisses, unwrapped**

Preheat oven to 350°. In a heavy saucepan over low heat, stir chocolate chips and butter until melted and smooth. Stir in sweetened condensed milk, flour and vanilla until well blended. Shape 1 level teaspoon of dough around each candy kiss. Arrange bonbons 1" apart on ungreased cookie sheets. Bake for 6 minutes. Bonbons will be soft and shiny, but will firm up as they cool.

Chocolate Peanut Butter Squares

Makes 3 dozen

1 C. butter or margarine
4 C. confectioners' sugar
2 C. peanut butter
1 1/2 C. graham cracker
   crumbs

1/2 C. butter or margarine
1 1/2 C. semisweet chocolate
   chips

Melt 1 cup butter over low heat, stirring constantly. Remove from heat and stir in confectioners' sugar, peanut butter and graham cracker crumbs. Spread mixture in a jelly roll pan. Pat down evenly. Melt together 1/2 cup butter with chocolate chips over low heat, stirring constantly. Spread chocolate over peanut butter mixture. Refrigerate for 1/2 hour. Cut into squares.

White Chocolate Covered Pretzels

Makes 16 servings

6-1 oz. squares white
    chocolate
1-15 oz. pkg. mini-twist
    pretzels

1/4 C. red and green candy
    sprinkles, optional

Melt white chocolate in the top of a double boiler, stirring constantly. Using a skewer, dip pretzels into the white chocolate, completely covering the pretzel. Roll in sprinkles if desired and lay on wax paper. Continue the process until all of the white chocolate is used. Place in refrigerator for 15 minutes to harden. Store in airtight container.

To remove tree sap from your hands, rub a bit of butter or oil into hands, wait a minute, then wipe off with a paper towel.

Cookie Bark

Makes 3 1/2 pounds

1-20 oz. pkg. chocolate sandwich cookies with cream filling

2-18.5 oz. pkgs. white chocolate

Line a 10x15" jelly roll pan with wax paper. Coat paper with non-stick vegetable spray and set aside. In a large mixing bowl, break half of the cookies into coarse pieces with fingers or the back of a wooden spoon. In a microwave safe glass mixing bowl, heat one package of the white chocolate in a microwave, stirring frequently, until melted and smooth. Remove from microwave and quickly fold in broken cookie pieces. Pour mixture into prepared pan and spread to cover half the pan. Repeat process with remaining chocolate and cookies, spreading mixture into the other half of pan. Refrigerate until solid, about 1 hour. Remove bark from the pan and carefully peel off wax paper. Place bark on a large cutting board and cut with a large chef's knife. Store in airtight container.

Santa's Favorite

Cookies

Four Spice Crackles

Makes 4 dozen

2 1/2 C. all-purpose flour
1 tsp. baking powder
1/2 tsp. baking soda
1/4 tsp. salt
1 1/2 tsp. ground ginger
1 tsp. ground cloves
1 tsp. ground nutmeg
3/4 tsp. ground cinnamon

1 C. packed brown sugar
1/2 C. unsalted butter,
  softened
1/2 C. shortening
1/4 C. molasses
1 egg
2/3 C. coarse granulated
  sugar

Sift together the flour, baking powder, baking soda, salt, ginger, cloves, nutmeg and cinnamon. Set aside. In a medium bowl, cream together the brown sugar, butter and shortening. Stir in the molasses and egg. Gradually stir in the dry ingredients until everything is incorporated. Cover and chill dough for at least 1 1/2 hours. Preheat oven to 350°. Lightly grease cookie sheets. Roll the chilled dough into 1" balls. Roll each ball in sugar. Place cookies 2" apart on the prepared cookie sheets and flatten slightly. Bake for 9 to 12 minutes until cookies are cracked but still soft in the center. Place cookies on wire racks to cool. Store cooled cookies in an airtight container.

White Chocolate & Cranberry Cookies

Makes 2 dozen

1/2 C. butter, softened
1/2 C. packed brown sugar
1/2 C. sugar
1 egg
1 T. apricot syrup
   or 1 tsp. apricot extract

1 1/2 C. all-purpose flour
1/2 tsp. baking soda
3/4 C. white chocolate chips
1 C. dried cranberries

Preheat oven to 375°. Grease cookie sheets. In a large bowl, cream together the butter, brown sugar and sugar until smooth. Beat in the egg and apricot syrup. Combine the flour and baking soda; stir into the sugar mixture. Mix in the white chocolate chips and cranberries. Drop by heaping spoonfuls onto prepared cookie sheets. Bake for 8 to 10 minutes. For best results, take cookies out while they are still doughy. Allow cookies to cool for 1 minute on the cookie sheets before transferring to wire racks to cool completely.

Reuse old Christmas cards fronts by writing thank you's in the format of a postcard. Postcard postage will also save you a few pennies.

Old Fashioned Sugar Cookies

Makes 6 1/2 dozen

3 C. sifted all-purpose flour
1 1/2 tsp. baking powder
1/2 tsp. salt
1 C. sugar

1 C. butter, softened
1 egg, lightly beaten
3 T. cream
1 tsp. vanilla extract

Preheat oven to 400°. In a large bowl, sift together all-purpose flour, baking powder, salt and sugar. Cut in butter and blend with a pastry blender until mixture resembles cornmeal. Stir in lightly beaten egg, cream and vanilla. Blend well. Dough may be chilled, if desired. On a floured surface, roll out dough to 1/8" thickness. Cut into desired shapes. Transfer to ungreased baking sheets. Bake for 6 to 8 minutes or until delicately browned. Watch closely!

Icing for Sugar Cookies:
6 1/2 C. confectioners' sugar
4 to 5 T. milk

4 to 5 T. light corn syrup
1 3/4 tsp. almond extract

In a small bowl, stir together confectioners' sugar and milk until smooth. Beat in corn syrup and almond extract until icing is smooth and glossy. If icing is too thick, add more corn syrup. Divide into separate bowls and add food colorings to each to desired intensity.

Mini Pecan Tarts

Makes 2 dozen

1/2 C. butter, softened	1 egg
1-3 oz. pkg. cream cheese, softened	3/4 C. packed brown sugar
	1 T. margarine, melted
1 C. all-purpose flour	1/2 C. chopped pecans

Preheat the oven to 325°. Beat butter and cream cheese until thoroughly combined. Stir in flour. Using 24 ungreased mini muffin cups, press a rounded teaspoon of pastry evenly into the bottom and up the sides of each cup. To make the filling, beat the egg and mix with brown sugar, melted butter and the chopped pecans. Fill each pastry-lined muffin cup with about 1 heaping teaspoon of pecan filling. Bake for approximately 30 minutes or until pastry is golden and filling is puffed. Cool tarts slightly in the muffin cups, then remove and cool completely on a wire rack.

Apricot Cream Cheese Thumbprints

Makes 7 dozen

1 1/2 C. butter, softened
1 1/2 C. sugar
1-8 oz. pkg. cream cheese, softened
2 eggs
2 T. lemon juice

1 1/2 tsp. lemon zest
4 1/2 C. all-purpose flour
1 1/2 tsp. baking powder
1 C. apricot preserves
1/3 C. confectioners' sugar

In a large bowl, cream together the butter, sugar and cream cheese until smooth. Beat in the eggs, one at a time, then stir in the lemon juice and lemon zest. Combine the flour and baking powder; stir into the cream cheese mixture until just combined. Cover, and chill until firm, about 1 hour. Preheat oven to 350°. Roll tablespoonfuls of dough into balls. Place dough balls 2" apart on ungreased cookie sheets. Using your finger, make an indentation in the center of each ball and fill with 1/2 teaspoon of apricot preserves. Bake for 15 minutes or until cookie edges are golden. Allow cookies to cool on the baking sheets for 2 minutes before removing to wire racks to cool completely. Sprinkle with confectioners' sugar.

Traditional Gingerbread Men

Makes 5 dozen

1 C. sugar
2 tsp. ground ginger
1 tsp. ground nutmeg
1 tsp. ground cinnamon
1/2 tsp. salt
1 1/2 tsp. baking soda

1 C. margarine, melted
1/2 C. evaporated milk
1 C. unsulfured molasses
3/4 tsp. vanilla extract
3/4 tsp. lemon extract
4 C. unbleached
    all-purpose flour

Preheat oven to 375°. Lightly grease cookie sheets. In a large bowl, stir together the sugar, ginger, nutmeg, cinnamon, salt and baking soda. Mix in the margarine, evaporated milk, molasses, vanilla and lemon extract. Stir in the flour, 1 cup at a time, mixing well after each addition. The dough should be stiff enough to handle without sticking to fingers. If necessary, increase flour by up to 1/2 cup to prevent sticking. When the dough is smooth, roll it out to 1/4" thick on a floured surface, and cut into desired shapes. Place cookies on the prepared cookie sheets. Bake for 10 to 12 minutes. The cookies are done when the top springs back when touched. Remove from cookie sheets to cool on wire racks.

Oatmeal Caramel Bars

Makes 24 servings

1-14 oz. pkg. caramels,
  unwrapped
1/2 C. evaporated milk
2 C. all-purpose flour
2 C. quick cooking oats
1 1/2 C. packed brown sugar

1 tsp. baking soda
1/2 tsp. salt
1 C. butter, melted
2 C. semisweet chocolate
  chips
1 C. chopped walnuts

Preheat oven to 350°. Grease a 9x13" baking pan. In a saucepan over medium heat, melt the caramels with the evaporated milk, stirring frequently until smooth. Set aside. In a medium bowl, stir together the flour, oats, brown sugar, baking soda and salt. Stir in the melted butter. Press half of the mixture into the bottom of the prepared pan. Bake for 10 minutes in the preheated oven. Remove from the oven and sprinkle the crust evenly with the chocolate chips and walnuts. Drizzle the caramel mixture over all. Crumble the remaining oat mixture evenly over the top, and pat down lightly. Bake for an additional 15 to 20 minutes or until the top is golden. Cool before cutting into bars.

Angel Crisps

Makes 3 dozen

1/2 C. sugar
1/2 C. packed brown sugar
1/2 C. shortening
1/2 C. butter
1 egg
1 tsp. vanilla extract

2 C. all-purpose flour
1 tsp. baking soda
1 tsp. cream of tartar
1/2 C. finely chopped
  walnuts
1/3 C. coarse granulated
  sugar

Preheat oven to 350°. Cream together the sugar, brown sugar, shortening and butter until smooth. Stir in the egg and vanilla. Sift together the flour, baking soda and cream of tartar. Stir into the sugar mixture. Roll dough into walnut-sized balls. Roll the balls in chopped nuts then in sugar. Place on ungreased cookie sheets and bake for 12 to 15 minutes or until cookies are light brown. Transfer cookies to a wire rack to cool.

For a clever way to give away cookies, stack and wrap them in clear cellophane, then tie and wrap each end with Christmas ribbon.

Almond Joy Cookies

Makes 2 dozen

1/2 C. butter, softened	1 tsp. baking soda
3/4 C. sugar	1/2 tsp. salt
3/4 C. packed brown sugar	2 C. semisweet chocolate
2 eggs	chips
2 tsp. vanilla extract	1 C. flaked coconut
2 1/4 C. all-purpose flour	1 C. chopped almonds

Preheat oven to 375°. Grease cookie sheets. In a large bowl, cream together the butter, sugar and brown sugar until smooth. Beat in the eggs, one at a time, then stir in the vanilla. Combine the flour, baking soda and salt, stir into the creamed mixture until well blended. Finally, stir in the chocolate chips, coconut and almonds. Drop by rounded spoonfuls onto the prepared cookie sheets. Bake for 8 to 10 minutes. Allow cookies to cool on baking sheets for 5 minutes before removing to a wire rack to cool completely.

Lemon Bars

Makes 36 servings

1 1/2 C. all-purpose flour
2/3 C. confectioners' sugar
3/4 C. butter or margarine,
    softened
3 eggs

1 1/2 C. sugar
3 T. all-purpose flour
1/4 C. lemon juice
1/3 C. confectioners' sugar

Preheat the oven to 375°. Grease a 9x13" baking pan. Combine the flour, 2/3 cup confectioners' sugar and butter. Pat dough into prepared pan. Bake for 20 minutes, until slightly golden. While the crust is baking, whisk together eggs, sugar, flour and lemon juice until frothy. Pour lemon mixture over the hot crust. Return bars to the preheated oven for an additional 20 to 25 minutes or until light golden brown. Cool on a wire rack. Dust the top with confectioners' sugar. Cut into squares.

Applesauce Cookies

Makes 5 dozen

1 C. packed brown sugar
3/4 C. shortening
1 egg
1 C. applesauce
2 1/2 C. all-purpose flour
1/2 tsp. baking soda

1/2 tsp. salt
3/4 tsp. ground cinnamon
1/4 tsp. ground nutmeg
1/4 tsp. ground cloves
1 C. chopped walnuts
1 C. raisins

Preheat the oven to 325°. Grease cookie sheets. In a medium bowl, cream together the brown sugar and shortening until smooth. Stir in egg and then the applesauce until well blended. Combine flour, baking soda, salt, cinnamon, nutmeg and cloves; stir into the applesauce mixture. Fold in walnuts and raisins. Drop by teaspoonfuls onto the prepared cookie sheets. Bake for 10 to 12 minutes, until cookie edges start to brown. Cool on cookie sheets for a few minutes before removing to wire racks to cool completely.

Raspberry Coconut Bars

Makes 2 dozen

1 1/4 C. flour
1/4 tsp. salt
1/2 C. butter or margarine
3 T. cold water

2 eggs
1/2 C. sugar
2 2/3 C. coconut
1/3 C. red raspberry
preserves

Heat oven to 425°. Mix flour and salt in medium bowl. Cut in butter until coarse crumbs form. Sprinkle water over mixture while tossing to blend well. Press evenly onto bottom of ungreased 9" square pan. Bake for 20 minutes or until lightly browned. Decrease oven temperature to 350°. Beat eggs in large bowl with electric mixer on high speed. Gradually add sugar, beating until thick and light in color. Fold in coconut. Spread preserves over crust to within 1/4" of edges. Carefully spread coconut mixture over preserves. Bake for 25 minutes or until golden brown. Cool completely on a wire rack. Cut into squares.

Never put away cookies that are not completely cool.

Constructing Gingerbread

Constructing a gingerbread house can be lots of fun, but be sure to plan more than one day to complete your gingerbread cabin. First, decide on a design, buy the ingredients and gather the supplies that will be needed (icing bags, tips and a covered tray). The second step is to bake your building pieces and allow them to completely cool before constructing your base (use cans of fruits and vegetables to hold the walls in place while the icing dries). Let the base dry overnight, and then assemble the roof. Allow another day for the roof's frosting to dry to ensure a sturdy gingerbread house. Finally, its time to decorate!

Use your imagination when it comes to decorating. Creativity and variety is the key. Consider buying small bags of candy or candy by the pound. Some favorite gingerbread house decorations are:

* Confectioners' sugar for snow
* Graham crackers for a door
* Necco wafers (a flat, round, old-fashioned candy in assorted colors that is sold in rolls) for roof shingles
* Sticks of gum for roof shingles
* Caramels, stacked cookies or candies for a chimney
* Candy canes for porch supports
* Vanilla wafers or crushed nuts for a walkway
* Cinnamon sticks, straight pretzels or tootsie rolls for firewood
* Peppermint candies, M&M's, Lifesavers, gum drops, red cinnamon candies, Chiclets, red and black licorice bites, rope or twists and candy canes for accents around the house

Building Gingerbread

Makes 1 gingerbread house

5 C. all-purpose flour*	**1 C. sugar**
1 tsp. baking soda	**1 C. molasses**
1 tsp. salt	**2 1/2 C. confectioners' sugar**
1 tsp. ground nutmeg	**1/4 tsp. cream of tartar**
1 T. ground ginger	**2 egg whites**
1 C. shortening	**1/2 tsp. vanilla extract**

Preheat the oven to 375°. Melt shortening in a large saucepan. Mix in sugar and molasses. Combine the flour, baking soda, salt, nutmeg and ginger; gradually stir into the sugar mixture, using your hands to work in the last bit. Dough should be stiff. On a floured surface, roll out dough to 1/4" to 3/8" thickness. Using a pizza cutter, cut dough shapes as desired. Make sure the gingerbread is of uniform thickness, or the edges may burn before the center is done. Place dough shapes onto cookie sheets. Bake for 13 to 15 minutes. Let cool for several minutes on the cookie sheet, then remove to racks to finish cooling. To make the frosting cement, mix together confectioners' sugar and cream of tartar in a medium bowl. Add egg whites and vanilla. Beat on high speed until frosting holds its shape. If necessary, add more confectioners' sugar to thicken the icing. Cover frosting with a damp cloth to prevent drying.

*Be sure to measure flour carefully. Use a spoon to scoop it into the cup, then level off top.

Chocolate Kiss Cookies

Makes 3 dozen

1 C. margarine, softened
1/2 C. sugar
1 tsp. vanilla extract
1 3/4 C. all-purpose flour

1 C. finely chopped walnuts
1-6 oz. bag milk chocolate
   candy kisses
1/3 C. confectioners' sugar

In a large bowl, cream margarine with sugar and vanilla until light and fluffy. Mix in flour and walnuts, beating on low speed until well mixed. Cover and refrigerate dough for 2 hours or until firm enough to handle. Preheat oven to 375°. Remove wrappers from chocolate kisses. Shape approximately 1 tablespoon of dough around each chocolate kiss; be sure to cover chocolate completely. Place cookies on an ungreased cookie sheet. Bake for 10 to 12 minutes. While cookies are still warm, roll them in confectioners' sugar.

Cranberry Orange Cookies

Makes 4 dozen

1 C. butter, softened
1 C. sugar
1/2 C. packed brown sugar
1 egg
1 tsp. orange zest
2 T. orange juice
2 1/2 C. all-purpose flour
1/2 tsp. baking soda

1/2 tsp. salt
2 C. chopped cranberries
1/2 C. chopped walnuts, optional
1/2 tsp. orange zest
3 T. orange juice
1 1/2 C. confectioners' sugar

Preheat the oven to 375°. In a large bowl, cream together the butter, sugar and brown sugar until smooth. Beat in the egg until well blended. Mix in 1 teaspoon orange zest and 2 tablespoons orange juice. Combine the flour, baking soda and salt; stir into the sugar mixture. Mix in cranberries and walnuts. Drop rounded tablespoonfuls of dough 2" apart onto ungreased cookie sheets. Bake for 12 to 14 minutes, until the edges are golden. Remove from cookie sheets to cool on wire racks. In a small bowl, mix together 1/2 teaspoon orange zest, 3 tablespoons orange juice and confectioners' sugar until smooth. Spread over the tops of cooled cookies. Let stand until set.

Peanut Butter Cup Cookies

Makes 40 cookies

1 3/4 C. all-purpose flour
1/2 tsp. salt
1 tsp. baking soda
1/2 C. butter, softened
1/2 C. sugar
1/2 C. peanut butter

1/2 C. packed brown sugar
1 egg, beaten
1 tsp. vanilla extract
2 T. milk
40 miniature peanut butter
   cups, unwrapped

Preheat oven to 375°. Sift together the flour, salt and baking soda; set aside. Cream together the butter, sugar, peanut butter and brown sugar until fluffy. Beat in the egg, vanilla and milk. Stir in the flour mixture; mix well. Shape dough into 40 balls. Place each cookie into an ungreased mini muffin pan. Bake for 8 minutes. Be careful not to over bake. Remove from oven and immediately press a mini peanut butter cup into each ball. Cool and carefully remove from pan.

Cherry Cordial Cookies

Makes 4 dozen

1 pkg. (about 18 oz.) cherry cake mix
3/4 C. butter or margarine, softened
2 eggs

1 C. semisweet mini chocolate chips
1 C. semisweet mini chocolate chips
3 T. shortening, no substitutions

Heat oven to 350°. In a large bowl, combine cake mix, butter and eggs; beat well. Stir in 1 cup mini chocolate chips. Drop by rounded teaspoonfuls onto ungreased cookie sheets. Bake for 10 to 12 minutes or until almost set. Cool for a few minutes on cookie sheets before removing to wire rack. Cool completely. To make glaze, in small microwave-safe bowl, place mini chocolate chips with shortening. Microwave on high for 45 seconds; stir. If necessary, microwave on high for an additional 15 seconds or until chocolate is melted and mixture is smooth when stirred. Immediately drizzle mini chips glaze onto cooled cookies; allow to set.

Store small Christmas ornaments in an egg carton.

101

Spritz Cookies

Makes 6 dozen

1 C. butter-flavored shortening
1-3 oz. pkg. cream cheese,
   softened
1 C. sugar
1 egg yolk

1 tsp. vanilla extract
1 tsp. orange zest
2 1/2 C. all-purpose flour
1/2 tsp. salt
1/4 tsp. ground cinnamon

Preheat oven to 350°. In a medium bowl, cream together shortening, cream cheese and sugar. Beat in egg yolk, vanilla and orange zest. Continue beating until light and fluffy. Gradually stir in flour, salt and cinnamon. Fill a cookie press and form cookies onto an ungreased cookie sheet. Bake for 10 to 12 minutes. Remove from cookie sheet and cool on wire racks.

Butter Pecan Squares

Makes 16 servings

1/2 C. butter, softened
1/2 C. packed brown sugar
1 egg
1 tsp. vanilla extract

3/4 C. all-purpose flour
2 C. milk chocolate chips,
divided
3/4 C. chopped pecans,
divided

Preheat oven to 350°. Grease an 8 or 9" square baking pan. Beat butter, brown sugar, egg and vanilla in a medium bowl until fluffy; stir in flour. Stir in 1 cup milk chocolate chips and 1/2 cup pecans. Spread batter evenly into prepared pan. Bake for 25 to 30 minutes or until lightly browned. Remove from oven. Immediately sprinkle remaining 1 cup milk chocolate chips over surface. Let stand 5 to 10 minutes or until chips soften; spread evenly. Immediately sprinkle remaining 1/4 cup pecans over top; press gently into chocolate. Cool bars completely in pan on wire rack. Cut into squares.

Chocolate Orange Cookies

Makes 3 dozen

1-1 oz. square unsweetened
   chocolate
3/4 C. butter
3/4 C. sugar
1 egg

1 tsp. vanilla extract
1 1/2 C. all-purpose flour
1 tsp. baking powder
1 pinch salt
1 T. orange zest

Preheat oven to 350°. In a medium bowl, cream together the butter and sugar until smooth. Beat in the egg and vanilla. Combine the flour, baking powder and salt; stir into the creamed mixture. Divide dough in two. In a microwave-safe dish, heat the unsweetened chocolate, stirring frequently until melted and smooth. Mix melted chocolate into one half of the dough and orange zest into the other half. Use a bit of each mixture to form a 1" ball. Bake for 8 to 10 minutes or until center is set. Transfer cookies to cool on a wire rack.

Caramel Filled Chocolate Cookies

Makes 4 dozen

1 C. butter, softened
1 C. sugar
1 C. packed brown sugar
2 eggs
2 tsp. vanilla extract
2 1/4 C. all-purpose flour
1 tsp. baking soda

3/4 C. unsweetened cocoa powder
1 C. chopped walnuts, divided
1 T. sugar
48 chocolate-covered caramel candies

Beat butter until creamy. Gradually beat in 1 cup sugar and brown sugar. Beat in eggs and vanilla. Combine flour, baking soda and cocoa. Gradually add to butter mixture, beating well. Stir in 1/2 cup walnuts. Cover and chill at least 2 hours. Preheat oven to 375°. Combine remaining 1/2 cup nuts with the 1 tablespoon sugar. Divide the dough into 4 parts. Work with one part at a time, leaving the remainder in the refrigerator until needed. Divide each part into 12 pieces. Quickly shape dough pieces around 12 chocolate covered caramels. Roll into a ball. Dip the tops into the sugar mixture. Place sugar side up, 2" apart on greased baking sheets. Repeat process with remaining dough parts. Bake for 8 minutes. Let cool for 3 to 4 minutes on the baking sheets before removing to wire racks to cool completely.

Saltine Toffee Cookies

Makes 35 servings

4 oz. saltine crackers
1 C. butter
1 C. dark brown sugar

2 C. semisweet chocolate chips
3/4 C. chopped pecans or walnuts

Preheat oven to 400°. Line cookie sheet with foil first. Line with saltine crackers in single layer. In a saucepan, combine the sugar and the butter. Bring to a boil and boil for 3 minutes. Immediately pour over saltines and spread to cover cracker completely. Bake at 400° for 5 to 6 minutes. Remove from oven and sprinkle chocolate chips over the top. Let sit for 5 minutes. Spread melted chocolate and top with chopped nuts. Cool completely and break into pieces.

Chocolate Cranberry Bars

Makes 18 servings

2 C. vanilla wafer crumbs
1/2 C. cocoa
3 T. sugar
2/3 C. cold butter, cut
   into pieces
1-14 oz. can sweetened
   condensed milk

1 C. peanut butter chips
1 1/3 C. (6 oz. pkg.)
   sweetened dried
   cranberries or
1 1/3 C. raisins
1 C. coarsely chopped
   walnuts

Heat oven to 350°. Stir together crumbs, cocoa and sugar in medium bowl; cut in butter until crumbly. Press mixture evenly on bottom and 1/2" up sides of 13x9x2" baking pan. Pour sweetened condensed milk evenly over crumb mixture; sprinkle evenly with peanut butter chips and dried cranberries. Sprinkle nuts on top; press down firmly. Bake 25 to 30 minutes or until lightly browned. Cool completely in pan on wire rack. Cover with foil; let stand several hours. Cut into bars.

Caramel Shortbread Squares

Makes 16 servings

2/3 C. butter, softened
1/4 C. sugar
1 1/4 C. all-purpose flour
1/2 C. butter
1/2 C. packed light brown
   sugar

2 T. light corn syrup
1/2 C. sweetened condensed
   milk
1 1/4 C. milk chocolate
   chips

Preheat oven to 350°. In a medium bowl, mix together 2/3 cup butter, 1/4 cup sugar and 1 1/4 cups flour until evenly crumbly. Press into greased and floured 9" square baking pan. Bake for 20 minutes. In a 2-quart saucepan, combine 1/2 cup butter, brown sugar, corn syrup and sweetened condensed milk. Bring to a boil. Continue to boil for 5 minutes. Remove from heat and beat vigorously with a wooden spoon for about 3 minutes. Pour over baked crust (warm or cool). Cool until it begins to firm. Melt chocolate and pour over caramel layer. Cover the layer completely. Chill. Cut into very small squares (about 48 - small because it is rich) before chocolate layer is completely set and remove from pan.

Holiday Wreaths

Makes 16 wreaths

1/3 C. butter
1-10.5 oz. pkg. large
  marshmallows

6 C. cornflakes cereal
1 tsp. green food coloring
1/4 C. cinnamon red hot
  candies

Melt margarine in a large pan over low heat. Add marshmallows and stir constantly until marshmallows melt and mixture is syrupy. Remove from heat. Stir in food coloring. Add cornflakes and stir until well coated. Drop mixture, by 1/4 cupful, onto cookie sheet. Using buttered fingers, quickly shape into individual wreaths. Dot with cinnamon candies.

Unfrosted cookies can be frozen for up to 12 months and frosted cookies can be frozen for up to 3 months if they are in an air-tight container.

Almond Snow Bars

Makes 16 servings

4 squares premium white
  baking chocolate
1/2 C. butter or margarine
3/4 C. sugar
2 eggs
1 tsp. almond extract

2/3 C. flour
1/2 tsp. baking powder
1/4 tsp. salt
3/4 C. chopped slivered
  almonds
Confectioners' sugar

Preheat oven to 350°. Line a 9" square baking pan with foil with ends of foil extending beyond edges of pan; grease foil. Microwave chocolate and butter in large microwavable bowl on high for 2 minutes or until butter is melted. Stir until chocolate is completely melted. Add sugar and mix well. Stir in eggs and almond extract. Add flour, baking powder and salt; mix well. Stir in almonds. Spread batter into prepared pan. Bake for 30 to 35 minutes or until golden brown. Cool in pan on wire rack. Sprinkle with confectioners' sugar. Lift bars out of pan onto a cutting board using ends of foil. Cut into squares.

Molasses Cookies

Makes 5 dozen

3/4 C. margarine, melted
1 C. sugar
1 egg
1/4 C. molasses
2 C. all-purpose flour
2 tsp. baking soda

1/2 tsp. salt
1 tsp. ground cinnamon
1/2 tsp. ground cloves
1/2 tsp. ground ginger
1/2 C. sugar

In a medium bowl, mix together the melted margarine, 1 cup sugar and egg until smooth. Stir in the molasses. Combine the flour, baking soda, salt, cinnamon, cloves and ginger; blend into the molasses mixture. Cover and chill dough for 1 hour. Preheat oven to 375°. Roll dough into walnut-sized balls and roll them in the remaining sugar. Place cookies 2" apart on ungreased baking sheets. Bake for 8 to 10 minutes, until tops are cracked. Cool on wire racks.

If you want to mail cookies, bar and soft cookies work the best. Avoid sending thin cookies or those with frostings or pointed edges.

Chewy Noels

Makes 1 1/2 dozen

2 T. butter
1 C. packed brown sugar
5 T. all-purpose flour
1/8 tsp. baking soda

2 eggs, beaten
1 tsp. vanilla extract
1 C. chopped walnuts
1/4 C. confectioners' sugar

Preheat oven to 350°. Melt the butter in a 9x13" baking dish. Ensure that all sides of the pan are coated; set aside. In a medium bowl, stir together the brown sugar, flour and baking soda. Mix in the eggs and vanilla until smooth, then stir in the walnuts. Pour over the melted butter. Bake for 20 minutes or until the edges begin to brown. Cool, then cut into squares and dust with confectioners' sugar.

Butter-Nut Kiss Cookies

Makes 2 1/2 dozen

1/2 C. butter or margarine,
    softened
1/2 C. sugar
1 egg
1 tsp. vanilla extract
1 1/4 C. all-purpose flour

1/4 tsp. baking soda
1/8 tsp. salt
30 chocolate kisses
1/2 C. ground almonds,
    pecans or walnuts

Beat butter, sugar, egg and vanilla in a medium bowl until well blended. Stir together flour, baking soda and salt; add to butter mixture, beating well. If necessary, refrigerate dough until firm enough to handle. Remove wrappers from chocolate kisses. Preheat oven to 350°. Shape dough into 1" balls; roll in ground nuts. Place on ungreased cookie sheets. Bake for 10 to 12 minutes or until almost no imprint remains when touched lightly in center. Remove from oven; immediately press a chocolate kiss into center of each cookie. Carefully transfer cookie to a wire rack. Cool completely. Chocolate should be set before storing.

Sugar Cookies

Makes 4 dozen

3 3/4 C. all-purpose flour
1 tsp. baking powder
1/2 tsp. salt
1 C. margarine, softened

1 1/2 C. sugar
2 eggs
2 tsp. vanilla extract

Sift flour, baking powder and salt together, set aside. In a large bowl, cream together the margarine and sugar until light and fluffy. Beat in the eggs one at a time, then stir in the vanilla. Gradually blend in the sifted ingredients until fully combined. Cover dough and chill for 2 hours. Preheat oven to 400°. Grease cookie sheets. On a clean floured surface, roll out small portions of chilled dough to 1/4" thickness. Cut out shapes using cookie cutters. Bake for 6 to 8 minutes or until edges are barely brown. Remove from cookie sheets to cool on wire racks.

Sugar Cookie Icing:

4 C. confectioners' sugar
2 to 3 T. milk

2 to 3 T. light corn syrup
1 tsp. almond extract

In a small bowl, mix confectioners' sugar and milk until smooth. Beat in corn syrup and almond extract until icing is smooth and glossy. If icing is too thick, add more corn syrup. Divide into separate bowls and add food colorings to each to desired intensity.

Peppermint Bars

Makes 2 dozen

1 C. butter
1 C. sugar
1 egg
1/4 tsp. peppermint extract
5 drops red food coloring
2 C. all-purpose flour

1/4 tsp. salt
1 C. semisweet chocolate chips
1/3 C. coarsely chopped peppermint candy canes

Preheat oven to 350°. Grease a 9x13" pan. Cream butter or margarine and sugar. Beat in egg, peppermint extract and food coloring. Add flour and salt until well blended. Spread evenly into greased pan. Bake for 25 minutes or until firm. After removing from oven, immediately sprinkle with chocolate chips. Cover pan with a cookie sheet for 1 minute or until chocolate is melted. Spread chocolate evenly and sprinkle with 1/3 cup coarsely chopped candy canes. Cool completely before cutting.

Recycle last year's Christmas cards by using them as gift tags. Cut out individual pictures or use the whole front cover.

Raspberry Oatmeal Bars

Makes 12 servings

1/2 C. packed brown sugar
1 C. all-purpose flour
1/4 tsp. baking soda
1/8 tsp. salt

1 C. rolled oats
1/2 C. butter, softened
3/4 C. seedless raspberry
    jam

Preheat oven to 350°. Grease an 8" square pan and line with greased foil. Combine brown sugar, flour, baking soda, salt and rolled oats. Cut in butter using a pastry blender to form a crumbly mixture. Press 2 cups of the mixture into the bottom of the prepared pan. Spread the jam to within 1/4" of the edges. Sprinkle the remaining crumb mixture over the top and lightly press it into the jam. Bake for 35 to 40 minutes or until lightly browned. Allow to cool before cutting into bars.

Chewy Chocolate-Cinnamon Cookies

Makes 40 cookies

6 T. butter or margarine,
   softened
2/3 C. packed brown sugar
3 T. plus 1/4 C. sugar,
   divided
1 egg
1 tsp. baking soda

1/4 C. light corn syrup
1 tsp. vanilla extract
1 1/2 C. all-purpose flour
1/3 C. unsweetened cocoa
   powder
1/4 to 1/2 tsp. ground
   cinnamon

Preheat oven to 350°. Grease cookie sheets. Beat butter until creamy. Add brown sugar and 3 tablespoons sugar; beat until blended. Add egg, baking soda, corn syrup and vanilla; beat well. Stir together flour and cocoa; beat into butter mixture. If batter is too stiff, use a wooden spoon. If necessary, cover and refrigerate for 30 minutes until batter is firm enough to shape. Shape dough into 1" balls. Combine 1/4 cup sugar and cinnamon; roll balls in mixture. Place balls 2" apart on prepared cookie sheet. Bake for 9 to 10 minutes or until cookies are set and tops are cracked. Cool slightly; remove from cookie sheet to wire rack. Cool completely.

Chewy Toffee Almond Bars

Makes 36 servings

1 C. butter, softened
1/2 C. sugar
2 C. all-purpose flour
1 3/4 C. (10 oz. pkg.) toffee
    bits

3/4 C. light corn syrup
1 C. sliced almonds, divided
3/4 C. coconut, divided

Preheat oven to 350°. Grease sides of 13x9x2" baking pan. Beat butter and sugar until fluffy. Gradually add flour, beating until well blended. Press dough evenly into prepared pan. Bake for 15 to 20 minutes or until edges are lightly browned. Meanwhile, combine toffee bits and corn syrup in medium saucepan. Cook over medium heat, stirring constantly, for approximately 10 to 12 minutes until toffee is melted. Stir in 1/2 cup almonds and 1/2 cup coconut. Spread toffee mixture to within 1/4" of edges. Sprinkle remaining 1/2 cup almonds and remaining 1/4 cup coconut over top. Bake for an additional 15 minutes or until bubbly. Cool completely in pan on wire rack. Cut into bars.

Chocolate Drop Sugar Cookies

Makes 1 dozen

2/3 C. butter, softened
1 C. sugar
1 egg
1 1/2 tsp. vanilla extract
1 1/2 C. all-purpose flour
1/2 C. unsweetened cocoa
   powder

1/2 tsp. baking soda
1/4 tsp. salt
1/3 C. buttermilk or sour
   milk*
Additional sugar

Preheat oven to 350°. Lightly grease cookie sheets. Beat butter and sugar in large bowl until well blended. Add egg and vanilla; beat until fluffy. Stir together flour, cocoa, baking soda and salt; add alternately with buttermilk to butter mixture. Drop tablespoonfuls of dough about 2" apart onto prepared cookie sheet. Bake for 13 to 15 minutes or until cookie springs back when touched lightly in center. Immediately sprinkle cookies lightly with additional sugar. Cool slightly; remove from cookie sheet to wire rack. Cool completely.

*To sour milk: Use 1 teaspoon white vinegar plus milk to equal 1/3 cup.

No-Molasses Gingerbread Men

Makes 2 1/2 dozen

1-3.5 oz. pkg. cook and serve
   butterscotch pudding mix
1/2 C. butter
1/2 C. packed brown sugar
1 egg

1 1/2 C. all-purpose flour
1/2 tsp. baking soda
1 1/2 tsp. ground ginger
1 tsp. ground cinnamon

In a medium bowl, cream together the dry butterscotch pudding mix, butter and brown sugar until smooth. Stir in the egg. Combine the flour, baking soda, ginger and cinnamon; stir into the pudding mixture. Cover and chill dough until firm, about 1 hour. Preheat oven to 350°. Grease baking sheets. On a floured board, roll dough out to about 1/8" thickness and cut into man shapes using a cookie cutter. Place cookies 2" apart on the prepared baking sheets. Bake for 10 to 12 minutes, until cookies are golden at the edges. Cool on wire racks.

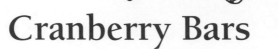

Cranberry Bars

Makes 24 servings

1-12 oz. pkg. whole cranberries	1 C. rolled oats
1 C. sugar	3/4 C. packed brown
3/4 C. water	sugar
1-18.25 oz. pkg. yellow cake mix	1 tsp. ground ginger
3/4 C. butter, melted	1 tsp. ground cinnamon
2 eggs	

In a saucepan over medium heat, combine the cranberries, sugar and water. Cook, stirring occasionally, until all of the cranberries have popped and the mixture is thick, about 15 minutes. Remove from heat and set aside to cool. Preheat oven to 350°. In a large bowl, mix the cake mix, melted butter and eggs. Stir in the oats, brown sugar, ginger and cinnamon. Set aside about 1 1/2 cups of the mixture and spread the rest into the bottom of a greased 9x13" baking dish. Pack down to form a solid crust, getting it as even as possible. Spread the cooled cranberry mixture over the crust. Pinch off pieces of the remaining mixture and place evenly over the cranberry layer. Bake for 35 to 40 minutes, until the top is lightly browned. Cool in the pan for at least an hour before slicing into bars.

Russian Tea Cakes

Makes 3 dozen

1 C. butter
1 tsp. vanilla extract
6 T. confectioners' sugar

2 C. all-purpose flour
1 C. chopped walnuts
1/3 C. confectioners' sugar

Preheat oven to 350°. In a medium bowl, cream butter and vanilla until smooth. Combine the 6 tablespoons confectioners' sugar and flour; stir into the butter mixture until just blended. Mix in the chopped walnuts. Roll dough into 1" balls and place them 2" apart on an ungreased cookie sheet. Bake for 12 minutes. When cooled, roll cookies in remaining confectioners' sugar.

Lemon Balls

Makes 4 dozen

1 1/2 C. sugar
1/2 C. shortening
3 eggs
1/2 tsp. vanilla extract
1/2 C. milk
1 tsp. lemon extract

3 C. all-purpose flour
3 tsp. baking powder
1 pinch salt
2 C. confectioners' sugar
3 T. water
1 tsp. lemon extract

Preheat oven to 350°. Blend the sugar and shortening until light and fluffy. Beat in the eggs, milk, vanilla and 1 teaspoon lemon extract. Mix until well blended. Combine the flour, baking powder and salt. Add the flour mixture to the shortening mixture. Mix until combined (the dough will be sticky). Drop spoonfuls of dough onto parchment paper lined baking sheets. Bake for 9 to 12 minutes. Let cookies cool, then frost with icing.

To Make Icing: Combine the confectioners' sugar, water and lemon extract to taste. Beat until smooth and make icing thick enough to spread on cooled cookies.

Keep wrapping paper from unrolling and getting crumpled by sliding an empty toilet paper roll that has been slit on one side around the tube of wrapping paper.

Chocolate Caramel Nut Bars

Makes 3 dozen

1 C. butter or margarine, softened

1/2 C. firmly packed brown sugar

2 C. flour

1/4 tsp. salt

1-12 oz. pkg. semi-sweet chocolate chunks

1-14 oz. pkg. individually wrapped caramels

1/3 C. whipping cream

1 C. chopped walnuts

Preheat oven to 350°. Beat butter and sugar in a large bowl on medium speed until light and fluffy. Add flour and salt; beat on low speed until crumbly. Press into 15x10" baking pan. Bake for 15 minutes or until edges are golden brown. Remove from oven. Sprinkle with chocolate chunks. Cover with foil. Let stand 5 minutes or until chocolate is melted. Spread chocolate evenly over top. Microwave unwrapped caramels and cream in microwavable bowl on high for 2 minutes or until caramels begin to melt. Stir in walnuts. Gently spread caramel mixture over chocolate. Cool in pan on wire rack. Cut into squares.

Santa's Favorite

Pies

Caramel Pecan Pie

Makes 1 pie

1-9" unbaked pie crust	**3/4 C. sugar**
36 individually wrapped	**3 eggs**
caramels, unwrapped	**1/2 tsp. vanilla extract**
1/4 C. butter	**1/4 tsp. salt**
1/4 C. milk	**1 C. pecan halves**

Preheat oven to 350°. In a saucepan over low heat, combine caramels, butter and milk. Cook, stirring frequently, until smooth. Remove from heat and set aside. In a large bowl, combine sugar, eggs, vanilla and salt. Gradually mix in the melted caramel mixture. Stir in pecans. Pour filling into unbaked pie crust. Bake for 45 to 50 minutes or until pastry is golden brown. Allow pie to cool until filling is firm.

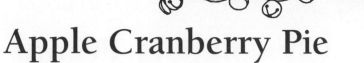

Apple Cranberry Pie

Makes 1 pie

1 1/4 C. white sugar
1/4 C. all-purpose flour
1/4 tsp. salt
2 C. cranberries
1/4 C. maple syrup
5 apples, peeled, cored
    and sliced

1/2 C. chopped walnuts
1-9" unbaked pie crust
1 C. dry bread crumbs
3/4 C. all-purpose flour
1/4 C. packed brown sugar
1/4 C. butter, melted

Preheat oven to 375°. In a large saucepan, mix together sugar, 1/4 cup flour and salt. Stir in cranberries and maple syrup. Cook over high heat, stirring constantly. When mixture comes to a boil, reduce heat, cover and simmer 5 minutes, stirring occasionally. Stir apples into simmering mixture and continue to cook for 5 minutes or until apples are tender. Remove from heat and stir in walnuts. Pour apple mixture into pie crust and set aside. In a medium bowl, combine bread crumbs, 3/4 cup flour, brown sugar and melted butter. Mix well and sprinkle over apple filling. Bake for 30 minutes or until topping is golden brown. Serve warm.

Chocolate & Peanut Butter Praline Pie

Makes 1 pie

3/4 C. packed brown sugar
1/2 C. sugar
3 T. all-purpose flour
2 eggs
1 T. milk
1 tsp. vanilla extract

1/3 C. butter or margarine, melted
1 C. pecan pieces
1/2 C. semisweet chocolate chips
1/2 C. peanut butter chips
1-9" unbaked pie crust

Preheat oven to 375°. Stir together brown sugar, sugar and flour in a medium bowl; beat in eggs, milk, vanilla and melted butter. Stir in pecan pieces, chocolate chips and peanut butter chips. Pour mixture into pie crust. Bake for 35 to 40 minutes or just until set and golden brown. Cool completely on wire rack.

Lemon Meringue Pie

Makes 1 pie

1-9" baked pie crust	4 eggs, separated
1 1/2 C. sugar	1/2 C. lemon juice
1/2 tsp. salt	2 tsp. lemon zest
1 1/2 C. water	3 T. butter or margarine
1/2 C. cornstarch	1/4 tsp. salt
1/3 C. water	1/2 C. sugar

Preheat oven to 325°. Combine 1 1/2 cups sugar, 1/2 teaspoon salt and 1 1/2 cups water in a heavy saucepan. Place over high heat and bring to a boil, stirring often. In a small bowl, mix cornstarch and 1/3 cup water to make a smooth paste. Gradually whisk into boiling sugar mixture. Boil mixture until thick and clear, stirring constantly. Remove from heat. In a small bowl, whisk together egg yolks and lemon juice. Gradually whisk egg yolk mixture into hot sugar mixture. Return pan to heat and bring to a boil, stirring constantly. Remove from heat and stir in lemon zest and butter. Place mixture in refrigerator and cool until just lukewarm. In a large glass or metal bowl, combine egg whites and 1/4 teaspoon salt. Whip until foamy. Gradually add 1/2 cup sugar while continuing to whip. Beat until stiff peaks form. Stir about 3/4 cup of meringue into lukewarm filling. Spoon filling into baked pastry shell. Cover pie with remaining meringue, being sure meringue touches crust edges. Bake for 15 minutes, until meringue is slightly brown. Cool on a rack for at least 1 hour before cutting.

Pumpkin Pie

Makes 1 pie

1-15 oz. can pumpkin puree
1-14 oz. can sweetened
  condensed milk
2 egg yolks
1 tsp. ground cinnamon
1/2 tsp. ground ginger
1/2 tsp. ground nutmeg
1/2 tsp. salt

2 egg whites
1-9" unbaked pie crust
2 T. all-purpose flour
1/4 C. packed brown sugar
1 tsp. ground cinnamon
2 T. butter, chilled
1 C. chopped walnuts

Preheat oven to 425°. In a large bowl, mix together the pumpkin, sweetened condensed milk and egg yolks. Stir in 1 teaspoon cinnamon, ginger, nutmeg and salt. In a large glass or metal bowl, whip egg whites until soft peaks form. Gently fold into pumpkin mixture. Pour filling into pie crust. Bake for 15 minutes. While the pie is baking, prepare the streusel topping. In a small bowl, combine the flour, brown sugar and 1 teaspoon cinnamon. Cut in the cold butter with a fork or pastry blender until the mixture is crumbly. Mix in the chopped nuts. Sprinkle the topping over the pie. Reduce oven temperature to 350°. Bake for an additional 40 minutes or until set.

Yummy Eggnog Pie

Makes 1 pie

1-4.6 oz. pkg. cook & serve
   vanilla pudding mix
1/4 tsp. ground nutmeg
1 1/2 C. eggnog

1/4 to 1/2 tsp. rum extract
2 C. heavy cream
1-9" baked pie crust
1 pinch ground nutmeg

In a medium saucepan, combine pudding mix, 1/4 teaspoon nutmeg and eggnog; mix well. Cook over medium heat, stirring constantly, until thick and bubbly. Remove from heat and stir in rum extract. Transfer mixture to a large bowl, cover and refrigerate until thoroughly chilled. In a medium bowl, whip the cream to soft peaks. Remove the cold pudding mixture from the refrigerator and beat until smooth; fold in whipped cream. Spoon into baked pie crust. Sprinkle additional nutmeg over the top for garnish. Refrigerate for 4 hours or until set.

A great gift for hard-to-buy-for-seniors is a large print calendar that highlights family member's birthdays and anniversaries.

Chocolate Walnut Pie

Makes 1 pie

6 T. butter or margarine
1/3 C. unsweetened cocoa
powder
1-14 oz. can sweetened
condensed milk
1/2 C. water

2 eggs, beaten
1/2 tsp. vanilla extract
1/2 tsp. imitation maple
flavor
1 C. coarsely chopped
walnuts
1-9" unbaked pie crust

Preheat oven to 350°. Melt butter in a medium saucepan over low heat. Add cocoa and stir until smooth. Stir in sweetened condensed milk, water and eggs; beat with whisk until well blended. Remove from heat; stir in vanilla, maple flavor and walnuts. Pour into pie crust. Bake for 40 to 45 minutes or until center is set. Cool slightly. Serve warm or cold. Refrigerate leftover pie.

Cranberry Crumb Pie

Makes 1 pie

1-9" unbaked pie crust
1-8 oz. pkg. cream cheese, softened
1-14 oz. can sweetened condensed milk
1/4 C. lemon juice
3 T. brown sugar, divided
2 T. cornstarch
1-16 oz. can whole berry cranberry sauce
1/4 C. butter, chilled and diced
1/3 C. all-purpose flour
3/4 C. chopped walnuts

Preheat oven to 425°. Bake unbaked pie crust for 8 minutes. Remove from heat. Reduce oven temperature to 375°. In a large bowl, beat cream cheese until fluffy. Mix in sweetened condensed milk until the mixture is smooth. Stir in lemon juice. Transfer mixture to pie crust. In a small bowl, mix 1 tablespoon brown sugar and cornstarch. Mix in whole berry cranberry sauce. Spoon the mixture evenly over the cream cheese mixture. In a medium bowl, mix butter, all-purpose flour and remaining brown sugar until crumbly. Stir in the walnuts. Sprinkle evenly over the cranberry mixture. Bake for 45 minutes or until bubbly and lightly browned. Cool on a wire rack. Serve at room temperature, or chill in the refrigerator.

Traditional Pecan Pie

Makes 1 pie

1 C. white corn syrup
1 C. packed brown sugar
1/3 tsp. salt
1/3 C. butter or margarine,
** melted**

3 eggs
1 C. chopped pecans
1-9" unbaked pie crust

Preheat oven to 350°. Combine corn syrup, brown sugar, salt and melted butter or margarine. Slightly beat the eggs and add to sugar mixture. Beat well and pour into unbaked pie crust. Arrange pecans evenly over top. Bake for 50 to 60 minutes. After 30 minutes, cover crust with foil to prevent it from getting too dark. Cool pie on wire rack before serving.

Sour Cream Raisin Pie

Makes 1 pie

1-9" baked pie crust
4 1/2 tsp. cornstarch
1 C. plus 2 T. sugar
1/4 tsp. salt
3/4 tsp. ground nutmeg
1 1/2 C. sour cream
3 egg yolks, beaten

1 1/2 C. raisins
1 T. lemon juice
3 egg whites
1/4 tsp. cream of tartar
6 T. brown sugar
1/2 tsp. vanilla extract

Preheat oven to 400°. In a medium saucepan, mix together cornstarch, sugar, salt and nutmeg. Mix in sour cream. Add egg yolks, raisins and lemon juice. Stir until thoroughly combined. Cook mixture over medium heat, stirring constantly, until mixture thickens and boils. Boil, stirring constantly for 1 minute. Pour mixture into baked pie crust. In a large glass or metal bowl, beat together egg whites and cream of tartar until foamy. Add brown sugar, 1 tablespoon at a time, continuing to beat until whites are stiff and glossy. Beat in vanilla extract. Spread evenly over raisin filling, sealing meringue to crust edges. Bake for 10 minutes until delicately browned.

Buttery Cranberry Pie

Makes 1 pie

1-9" double pie crust
1 1/2 C. sugar
1/3 C. all-purpose flour
1/4 tsp. salt
1/2 C. water

1-12 oz. pkg. fresh
   cranberries
1/4 C. lemon juice
1 dash ground cinnamon
2 tsp. butter

Preheat oven to 425°. In a large saucepan, combine sugar, flour, salt and water. Bring to a boil and cook, stirring constantly until thick and smooth. Add cranberries, lemon juice and cinnamon. Cook for an additional 5 minutes until mixture is thick and cranberries pop. Remove from heat and stir in butter. Spoon filling into bottom of pie crust. Cut top crust into strips for lattice. Place lattice strips on top and seal edges. Bake for 40 minutes or until crust is golden brown.

Chocolate Cream Pie

Makes 1 pie

3/4 C. sugar
1/3 C. all-purpose flour
2 C. milk
2-1 oz. squares unsweetened
  chocolate, chopped

3 egg yolks
2 T. butter or margarine
1 tsp. vanilla extract
1-9" baked pie crust
Whipped topping

Combine sugar, flour, milk and chopped chocolate in a 2-quart saucepan. Cook over medium heat, stirring constantly, until mixture begins to boil. Continue stirring for 2 minutes. Mix a little of the hot mixture into the egg yolks, beating rapidly to avoid cooking the yolks. Stir the warm yolk mixture into the remainder of the chocolate mixture and cook for an additional 90 seconds. Remove from heat and stir in butter or margarine and vanilla. Pour filling into pie crust and chill until set. Top with whipped topping and garnish with grated chocolate.

Pumpkin Toffee Pie

Makes 1 pie

1-9" unbaked pie crust
3/4 C. toffee baking bits
1-15 oz. can pumpkin puree
1/2 C. sugar
1 C. packed brown sugar
1 1/2 tsp. ground cinnamon
1 tsp. ground ginger

1/2 tsp. ground nutmeg
1 tsp. vanilla extract
1 pinch salt
1/2 C. milk
1/2 C. heavy cream
3 eggs

Preheat oven to 375°. Sprinkle toffee bits into pie crust and set aside. In a large bowl, combine pumpkin puree, sugar, brown sugar, cinnamon, ginger, nutmeg, vanilla and salt. Beat in the milk, cream and eggs until filling is smooth and creamy. Pour filling over toffee bits in pie crust. Place on baking sheet in the middle of the oven. Bake for 60 to 90 minutes or until filling center is set. After 30 minutes, cover crust with foil to prevent it from getting too dark.

Creamy Cranberry Pie

Makes 1 pie

2/3 C. boiling water
1-4 oz. pkg. cranberry
   flavor gelatin
1/2 C. cold water
Ice cubes
1-8 oz. tub whipped topping

1 tsp. grated orange peel,
   optional
1 C. whole berry cranberry
   sauce
1 graham cracker pie crust

In a large bowl, stir boiling water into gelatin for at least 2 minutes until gelatin is completely dissolved. Mix cold water with enough ice to measure 1 cup. Add to gelatin, stirring until slightly thickened. Remove any remaining ice. Stir in whipped topping and orange peel with wire whisk until smooth. Gently stir in cranberry sauce. Refrigerate for 20 to 30 minutes or until mixture is very thick and will mound. Spoon filling into crust. Refrigerate for 4 hours or until firm. Store leftover pie in refrigerator.

To mail cookies, wrap in pairs, flat sides together using foil or plastic wrap. Ship in sturdy containers like tins, heavy cardboard or wooden boxes.

Chocolate Rum Mousse Pie

Makes 1 pie

1-.25 oz. pkg. unflavored
  gelatin
1 T. cold water
2 T. boiling water
1/2 C. sugar
1/4 C. unsweetened cocoa
  powder
1-3.9 oz. pkg. instant
  chocolate pudding mix

2 C. heavy cream, chilled
1 tsp. vanilla extract
1 tsp. rum flavored
  extract
1-9" chocolate cookie
  crumb crust
1 C. heavy cream, chilled
2 T. confectioners' sugar
1/2 tsp. rum flavored
  extract

In a small bowl, sprinkle gelatin onto cold water; let stand for
1 minute to soften. Stir in boiling water until gelatin is
completely dissolved. Gelatin mixture must be in liquid form
when mixed with pie filling. If it stiffens up, microwave for
about 10 to 15 seconds and then stir until lump free. In a large
bowl, combine sugar, cocoa and pudding mix. Stir in 2 cups
cream, vanilla and 1 teaspoon rum extract. Beat for 30 seconds
on low speed, and then beat on high until stiff peaks form.
Gradually mix in liquid gelatin mixture until well blended.
Pour filling into crumb crust. In a small bowl, beat 1 cup cream
with confectioners' sugar and 1/2 teaspoon rum extract until
stiff peaks form. Spread over chocolate filling. Chill for at least
2 hours before serving.

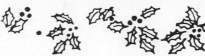

Pumpkin Chiffon Pie

Makes 1 pie

1 C. pumpkin puree	2 T. butter or margarine
3 eggs, separated	1-.25 oz. pkg. unflavored
1/2 C. sugar	gelatin
1 C. milk	1/4 C. cold water
1/2 tsp. salt	1/2 C. sugar
2 tsp. pumpkin pie spice	1-16 oz. pkg. gingersnap
	cookies

Line one 9" pie pan with whole gingersnap cookies, breaking as necessary for fitting. In a saucepan over medium heat, cook pumpkin puree to heat through, stirring frequently. Combine the egg yolks, 1/2 cup sugar, milk, salt, pumpkin pie spice and butter. Add to pumpkin and cook, stirring frequently, until mixture is of custard consistency. Remove mixture from heat. Soften gelatin in the cold water and stir into the pumpkin until dissolved. Chill mixture for about 1 1/2 hours until it begins to stiffen. Whip egg whites with the remaining 1/2 cup sugar until stiff. Fold whipped egg whites into the pumpkin mixture. Spoon mixture into the prepared pan and chill for about 3 hours until set. Serve topped with whipped cream.

Caramel Apple Pie

Makes 1 pie

1-9" double deep dish
   pie crust
1/2 C. packed brown sugar
1/4 C. butter or margarine,
   melted
1/3 C. all-purpose flour
5 C. thinly sliced apples

2/3 C. sugar
3 T. all-purpose flour
2 tsp. ground cinnamon
1 tsp. lemon juice
20 caramels, halved
2 T. milk

Preheat oven to 375°. To make taffy combine brown sugar, melted butter and 1/3 cup flour in a small bowl. Mix well and set aside. To make apple filling place apples in a large bowl. Add sugar, 3 tablespoons flour, cinnamon and lemon juice. Toss until all ingredients are mixed well and apples are thoroughly coated. Spoon half of apple filling into pastry-lined deep dish pie pan. Top with half of the halved caramels and half of the taffy mixture. Repeat process with remaining apple filling, caramels and taffy mixture. Place top pastry over filling and seal well (this is very important - if edges are not sealed completely, caramel will leak out all over). Cut steam vents and brush top crust with milk. Cover pie with foil and place on a baking sheet. Bake for 25 minutes. Remove foil from pie and bake for another 20 to 25 minutes, until crust is golden. Serve warm.

Sweet Potato Pie

Makes 1 pie

1-1 lb. sweet potato
1/2 C. butter, softened
1 C. sugar
1/2 C. milk
2 eggs

1/2 tsp. ground nutmeg
1/2 tsp. ground cinnamon
1 tsp. vanilla extract
1-9" unbaked pie crust

Boil sweet potato whole in skin for 40 to 50 minutes or until done. Run cold water over the sweet potato and remove the skin. Preheat oven to 350°. Break apart sweet potato in a bowl. Add butter and beat until mixed well. Stir in sugar, milk, eggs, nutmeg, cinnamon and vanilla. Beat on medium speed until mixture is smooth. Pour filling into an unbaked pie crust. Bake for 55 to 60 minutes or until a knife inserted in center comes out clean. Pie will puff up like a soufflé and then will sink down as it cools. After 30 minutes, cover crust with foil to prevent it from getting too dark.

To vacuum tree needles, put a pantyhose leg on the nozzle. Hold onto the hose around the nozzle while vacuuming. When done, pull out the pantyhose full of needles and throw away. No need to worry about a plugged up vacuum.

Toasted Coconut, Pecan and Caramel Pie

Makes 2 pies

2-9" baked pie crusts
1/4 C. butter
1-8 oz. pkg. flaked coconut
1/2 C. chopped pecans
1-8 oz. pkg. cream cheese,
   softened

1-14 oz. can sweetened
   condensed milk
1-12 oz. container
   whipped topping
1-12 oz. jar caramel
   ice cream topping

In a medium skillet, melt butter or margarine over medium heat. Add coconut and pecans. Toss well and sauté until coconut is lightly browned. Set aside to cool. In a large mixing bowl, beat cream cheese until fluffy. Add sweetened condensed milk and mix until smooth. Fold in whipped topping. Spread 1/4 of cream cheese mixture into each pastry shell. Sprinkle 1/4 of coconut mixture over each pie. Drizzle 1/2 of caramel topping over each coconut layer. Follow with remaining cream cheese mixture, then remaining coconut mixture. Pies may be served chilled or frozen.

Black Forest Pie

Makes 1 pie

4-1 oz. squares unsweetened
   baking chocolate,
   coarsely chopped
1-14 oz. can sweetened
   condensed milk
1 tsp. almond extract

1 1/2 C. cold whipping cream
1-9" baked pie crust
1-21 oz. can cherry pie filling,
   chilled
Toasted sliced almonds,
   optional

Combine chopped chocolate with sweetened condensed milk
in a heavy saucepan. Cook over medium heat, stirring
constantly, until chocolate is melted. Remove from heat and
stir in almond extract. Pour into a large bowl; refrigerate
until thoroughly cooled. Beat until smooth. Beat whipping
cream in medium bowl until stiff peaks form; gradually fold
into chocolate mixture. Pour into a baked pie crust.
Refrigerate for 4 to 6 hours or until set. Serve with cherry
pie filling. Garnish with toasted almonds, if desired. Cover
and refrigerate leftover pie.

Double Layer Pumpkin Pie

Makes 1 pie

4 oz. cream cheese, softened
1 T. milk
1 T. sugar
1 1/2 C. frozen whipped topping, thawed
1-9" graham cracker crust
1 C. cold milk

2-3.5 oz. pkgs. instant vanilla pudding mix
1-15 oz. can solid pack pumpkin puree
1 tsp. ground cinnamon
1/2 tsp. ground ginger
1/4 tsp. ground cloves

In a large bowl, whisk together cream cheese, milk and sugar until smooth. Gently stir in whipped topping. Spread into bottom of crust. Pour milk into large bowl and thoroughly mix in pudding mix, pumpkin, cinnamon, ginger and cloves. When thickened, spread over cream cheese layer. Refrigerate for 4 hours or until set.

Cranberry Nut Pie

Makes 1 pie

1 1/4 C. fresh or frozen cranberries	**1 egg**
1/4 C. brown sugar	**1/2 C. sugar**
1/4 C. chopped walnuts	**1/2 C. all-purpose flour**
	1/3 C. butter, melted

Preheat oven to 325°. Grease a 9" pie plate and layer cranberries on the bottom. Sprinkle with brown sugar and chopped walnuts. In a large bowl, beat egg until thick. Gradually add sugar, beating until thoroughly blended. Stir in flour and melted butter. Blend well and pour over cranberries. Bake for 45 minutes or until golden brown. Serve warm.

Fudgey Pecan Pie

Makes 1 pie

1/3 C. butter or margarine
2/3 C. sugar
1/2 C. unsweetened cocoa
    powder
3 eggs
1 C. light corn syrup
1/4 tsp. salt

1 C. chopped pecans
1-9" unbaked pie crust
1/2 C. cold whipping
    cream
1 T. confectioners'
    sugar
1/4 tsp. vanilla extract

Preheat oven to 375°. Melt butter in a medium saucepan over low heat. Add sugar and cocoa, stirring until well blended. Remove from heat and set aside. Beat eggs slightly in a medium bowl. Stir in corn syrup and salt. Add cocoa mixture and blend well. Stir in chopped pecans. Pour into unbaked pie crust. Bake for 45 to 50 minutes or until set. Cool. For a crispy top on pie, cool and serve. For a softer top on pie, cool and cover; let stand for about 8 hours before serving. Garnish with sweetened whipped cream and, if desired, pecans. To make sweetened whipped cream, stir together cold whipping cream, confectioners' sugar and vanilla in a small bowl. Beat until stiff peaks form.

INDEX

COOKIES

PIES

SNACKS